THE BIGGEST MISTAKE

Can cost you *Everything*

K. Lee

AuthorKLee.com

KLEPub.com

THE BIGGEST MISTAKE

Can cost you *Everything*

Published by Krystal Lee Enterprises (KLE Publishing)
Copyright © 2023 by K. Lee All rights reserved. Please send comments and questions:
Krystal Lee Enterprises
770-240-0089 Ext. 1
sales@KLEPub.com
To Reach the Author:
Email: me@authorklee.com or me@drkrystallee.com
Web: AuthorKLee.com
Social Media: @AuthorKLee

Printed in the United States of America.
All rights reserved. No part of this book may be reproduced or transmitted in any form or by any means, electronic or mechanical, including photocopying, recording or any information storage and retrieval system without written permission of the publisher except for brief quotations used in reviews, written specifically for inclusion in a newspaper, blog, magazine, or academic paper.

ISBN: 978-1-945066-19-1

D

DEDICATION

I want to thank Yah for giving me the assignment and grace to write and finish this book. Next, I want to thank my beautiful children, my mother, and niece Angel-Marie for helping me during the time of making this book. I also want to thank my siblings whom I love tremendously for always rooting for me, as well as my aunts, uncles, and grandparents. My good friend, Stan Foster for always pushing me and keeping me on my toes. My pastor Bishop Steven L Thompson, and Dr. Tyrone Bostic for supporting me. A special thanks to Southeren Theological Institute of Biblical Studies (STIBS) of Indiana. Lastly, I want to thank you the reader. May this book encourage you and your family.

K. Lee

T

TABLE OF CONTENTS

Foreward **6**

Introduction **10**

Kings **20**

    King Saul the Fallen King **21**

    Jonathan: The Faithful Servant **35**

Sons **58**

    Eli's Lost Battle: The Death of His Legacy **59**

    The Prodigal's Second Chance **76**

Deliverer **84**

    Moses, Pharoah, and Yah's Wrath **85**

    After the Sea **112**

Love **116**

    Samson's Deadly Love for the Forbidden **117**

    Hosea's Bond and Yah's mirrored marriage to a Whore **134**

Follow **152**

    A People After Yah's Own Heart **153**

About the Author **160**

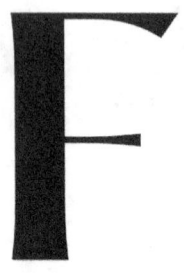

FOREWARD

We all live a life of decision. When the Creator of the Universe gave man dominion over the earth, He did so with a few laws of order. We were made in His image, His likeness, yielding the power to use words to shape our lives. With those words, we make choices in our mind that then translate to the physical realm.

What happens when we make the biggest mistake of our life? Can one decision really cost us everything? Is that fair for that to be the case for some of us and not all of us?

Truthfully, life is not fair. Every day we live with the choices each of us has made, both individually or by association, that could have diverse reactions on others. In the same way that parents' choices impact their children, our choices affect our legacy. In like manner, the people we vote into congress can make sweeping decisions that impact the nations.

Then the ultimate is how the choices of Christ to live and die for humanity to be reconciled to the Almighty Creator, has given His brothers and sisters in Christ access to the Almighty Yah (God). When He died on the cross the veil was torn allowing believers a closer relationship with the Father. Through His act of obedience, those that have not been faithful can be saved by pleading His righteousness and sacrifice over their sins.

We all love to benefit from actions we have not sown, but it can be a big challenge to bear each other's burdens when there are adverse effects. Dealing with generational curses because of a big mistake by a parent, uncle, relative, friend, or stranger can be very hard. We hate being accountable for what we have not done if it does not benefit us. Yet we live in a world where that appears to be the case.

Being a part of the church doesn't excuse us from having to make big decisions and live with our choices. For those that serve Yah, we understand, He will not force us to do anything (although He can be very convincing) we don't choose to do! We must choose to do right even in the face of adversity and that decision is always ours to make.

Many people in the Bible had to deal with issues, troubles, and circumstances that are not too different from what we go through today. The choice to do right, take the righteous path, approach us all, but we all don't make the same decisions as people in the Bible do we? Then to be fair, we can make the same decisions and get two different outcomes or consequences, right?

If your mind wasn't troubled before, it might be now, because there are differences among children in the Kingdom of God. King David's grace you may notice is not yours. Job's challenge, wasn't yours. You didn't lose your children, but you may have felt a test cost you your mind. Noah's favor might not be yours either. Some of us can't look at liquor without our world crumbling. Many believe drunks are not good for much more than they can supply, but God started creation over with a drunkard's family.

We may have a similar influence to Paul, but we don't suffer from the same thorn in our side as Paul. Maybe your issue isn't a physical illness, but something mental, emotional, social, etc. What is irrefutable is that we all struggle with at least one thorn that we will admit. Then who knows how many demons we fight that we either won't or can't place a name on.

I have noticed that as we journey with Yah we may falsely assume His power is ours. Sometimes circumstances give us a false sense of power. We may start with a humble beginning, but then something happens in us that makes us believe we have outgrown humility. I dare say pride shows up to cast out humility.

Consider this, can we ever actually pull off the concept of outgrowing our Master? Can we become wiser than our Teacher? Samuel was the prophet that anointed Saul, making him King of the Hebrews.

He was the first king and he represented the heart of the people. He was also a token of how fickle Yah's people were towards Him.

They loved Him when they were low, in want, and downtrodden in society. When they were the underdog, Yah smiled and showed favor to them. They realized their limitations caused them to need God! Some argue faith is only good for the weak and the poor. Do you believe that?

This logic of the poor being the only ones that need God couldn't be further from the truth and I want to tell you why in this book. Many believe—although they wouldn't admit it, love help when they are down. Yet something happens when certain people get money or rise above their circumstances. Some say they show the colors they always had, others would say they fell victim to the power of fame. This fact remains, the rich, the poor, the first, and the last are capable of making choices that in reality could cost them everything!

There are mistakes we can make that will alter our lives forever. We tend to think, I can make this mistake one time and do better the next time. But can you or anybody afford to be so sure? Sometimes,

even the first time, can be The Biggest Mistake that Can Cost You

Everything!

I

INTRODUCTION

In the United States, many are familiar with the first-time offender's program. It is no secret that some first-time offenders appear to receive very different treatment or outcomes than others. Arguably so, many people of color tend to get harsher punishments on their first offense compared to other nationalities.

We have all heard of accounts where young black men were charged as adults even though they were minors when they committed the offense. Is it fair that the treatment of one is not the treatment of all? Some judges would argue if the punishment is too light, the offender won't learn their lesson. With a mindset like this, that judge and others who think like him can justify giving longer terms for non-violent crimes.

These defendants may be on their first charge, their crimes might be non-violent, and yet they are receiving 5, 10, 15, or even 20 years. Others are being arrested alive after killing children, teenagers, or the elderly, and their punishments are lighter than those who have non-violent crimes. Many have come to realize when their son, daughter, mother, or father goes to jail or prison with time to be served like this on a first offense, life isn't fair.

I know of people who were handcuffed as soon as the police arrived because they were perceived to be a threat before an interrogation even ensued. I have heard of people getting arrested in front of their parents because they were accused of child abuse. I learned you can go to jail for raising your voice as a black man in front of your children because that is considered child abuse.

In another case, the man had eyewitnesses who saw what happened, but when the police showed up, they arrested him on the spot and came in like the SWAT! There were no guns, drugs, violence, or even yelling happening at the time. He was on his phone, standing by the stairs, and his parents were sitting watching television. The environment was calm, but the overkill of a pursuit dramatized a regular evening of black people sitting in the living room.

Nobody even knew the police were called. Come to find out, his girlfriend didn't want to leave his residence and said she was being held captive when, in fact, she wanted to stay, and he desired for her to leave. None of the witnesses were on the report or invited to the court dates. The case couldn't be canceled by the person who initiated it, and the only way out for him first appeared as a plea deal to become a felon for a crime he didn't commit.

If he didn't have the finances to fight his

charges and stand up for the truth, he, unfortunately, would have fallen victim as too many have for taking a plea deal. There is no denying if you cannot afford to fight jail time, you will likely end up serving jail time regardless of whether you are guilty or not. Because wrong time, bad circumstances, and the likelihood of you looking as if you committed a crime are enough for too many to convict you.

How are things like this possible? How is it possible that justice appears to be so lopsided? Can a mistake that seems small to one person really jump to become a life-altering experience? If you live in a community with limited resources or appear to fit the bill of what may be presumed the "type" who committed a crime, one would find judgment has already been cast against them and not in their favor.

I consider it strange how some people unconsciously assume the value of another person. I know a woman, Tiffany Small, who wrote the book *The False Police Report*, detailing her story with the Virginia Police Department. She lost 8 months of being in her child's life because she was bullied into taking a plea deal that made her a felon for the past 20-odd years.

This felony made her life a serious challenge, and a system that was meant to stand for justice, fairness, and balance would appear to be very biased considering the evidence that was present and "lost" in her case. It is amazing to me, and not in a good way, how we size up a few things on sight and make life-changing decisions based on them.

There are many factors that make this the case. We look to see someone's annual income to determine their sex appeal. We access their ability to make payments and be a good slave to a system built on debt and payments to determine credit scores. We also look at their clothes, house, car, general appearance, and credit score to determine if someone deserves mercy, advancement, respect, and the like.

Do you not think it odd that you have to wear a suit to court not because you want to be respectful or even because you like them? Many have been instructed to dress a certain way so the jury or judge doesn't prejudge them for their appearance. To me, that means the facts could be on the table, but if a person feels you are guilty, an innocent person can be put into jail or prison based on opinions.

Although this appears to be an unfair or jaded topic for many in light of recent events, we must discuss how one mistake can morph into ***The Biggest Mistake that Can Cost You Everything***! No one thinks about the consequences of getting caught for an offense more than the benefits. Many who decide to break into a person's home and steal their property don't dwell on getting caught.

They don't dwell on being found out, and many only consider it dangerous if the family is at home. Most thieves prefer for the homeowners not to be present, but not all! Some are so in love with the opportunity to get something for what they perceive as nothing they will fight or kill for it. A logical person may argue that a thief doesn't value hard work. If they only knew how hard a mother worked to buy her children a game system, tv, or expensive gadget, would they be so keen to take it? If the same thing were to happen to them, their entire house was cleaned out, would stealing be such a good idea?

Some steal from supermarkets, convenience stores, and other chains for the thrill. They don't like taking much but something—even if it holds no monetary value. A kleptomaniac falls in love with the energy, the false sense of power, of getting away with something. It is not the thing that matters but their perception of themselves.

Many laugh at a person with this kind of problem because they argue if you are going to steal, steal something worth taking. A question I would ask is, is there anything worth taking? Do we really believe we can get something for nothing? Can we really sow seeds of injustice, and nothing ever turns back on us as a judgment or repayment?

Likewise, some cheat because that person gave them something they didn't get at home, many say. My wife doesn't do this for me. "She doesn't cook, won't clean, and the house is just upside down. I work hard to pay the bills, and surely I am deserving of someone who is my equal."

"I am not going to leave her. I just want to show her that I can do better. Maybe cheating on her would help wake her up to how good of a man I am!" I have heard this argument in coaching. Have you heard it from your friends, or have you played the conversation in your own head?

Women are not any better. Some say they don't have a legitimate reason to cheat on their spouse. They confess, "He is a good man. He loves me, takes care of the children, cooks, cleans, works, and just wants to make me happy. I just have one problem, Krystal. He is boring, too safe, and doesn't make me feel wanted."

"Krystal, sometimes I just want a man that makes me feel different. I don't like that he is always nice to me. Sometimes, I just want somebody who would tell me to shut up or choke me a little bit! You know? Argue with me; do something that shows he has passion! An agreeable man is just, well, weak to me. I need a challenge."

She says, "Is it really wrong if I am good to him? I just step out from time to time to find that spark. I don't really want a man like this to marry, but he brings excitement to a boring life."

The thrill of the hunt doesn't just impact men, but women also want to feel this larger-than-life experience, *The Ecstasy*. They want Heavon but won't give up Hell to get it. This feeling makes them feel alive and vital to society in some way. There are women planning to have children, so their presence can be constant in a man's life even if he doesn't desire that. Is it fair for a trap to be laid, you unknowingly walk in it, then receive a harsh punishment for life?

Are you familiar with the law of entrapment? Entrapment is a complete defense to a criminal charge on the theory that "Government agents may not originate a criminal design, implant in an innocent person's mind to commit a criminal act, and then induce commission of the crime so that the Government may prosecute" (Justice.gov).

Have you heard people cry out entrapment when they are tempted? If she didn't wear that or if he didn't say that, this would have never happened. I was preyed upon, and my ignorance was used against me to bewitch or entangle me in this act. If I had a clear mind, if I wasn't hurt, abused, or needing affection, this wouldn't be possible. If only she or he met my needs, I wouldn't have needed to step out.

Remember how in Genesis, Adam said that Yah/God gave him this wife? It was as if God Almighty had given Adam something that was broken. The woman was made perfect, as was he, but they both made The Biggest Mistake that cost humanity Everything! It wasn't three strikes, and you're out. It wasn't a "control z" keystroke they could hit to reverse time.

They couldn't get a redo or a warning. Their charge and consequence for one action cost us all! So, if we have this colorful example set before all humanity really got into motion, how is it that we have not perceived and accepted the truth that the biggest mistake can cost you everything?

How can we have the confidence or ability to make such a decision and expect no fallout from our decisions? How can we make choices and not consider the long-term effects? How can we sin against our own bodies and call it good? How do we steal from our neighbors and expect no one to take from us?

Why do we think we can lust after someone's wife or husband, even if they may be single now? We don't know the future of that person's life. They may not be married today, but the Father knows who will be married tomorrow! To make matters worse, for the one who is not single today, how great the shame.

A believer doesn't have a picture-perfect life. Many who are believers can attest they have made some of these choices knowing Yah/God was there looking over their shoulder. We can have the form of godliness and the power of Yah be far from us (*2 Timothy 3:5*).

Now, a core subject of this book is King Saul and King David. Mercy looked very different for each of their lives. They both made bad decisions, but their outcomes were different.

When we are on the path Yah has for us, we are in His presence. His Spirit and presence are accompanied by giftings and a calling that helps you to execute a divine assignment. Whether that be a kingship anointing, prophetic, teaching, preaching, serving, defending, or other, God gives you what you need to accomplish your purpose.

Regardless of whether you are living right or wrong, your assignment is set before you arrive here on Earth. The Bible says in *Jeremiah 1:5*, "Before I formed you in the womb I knew you, and before you were born I consecrated you; I appointed you a prophet to the nations." Before we chose the life Yah/God has set up for us, the plan was already in place concerning what He intended for us. Jeremiah was called to be a prophet, and the only way for him to know was to go to God and find out.

All believers have access to the throne room of grace. When you are born again, your gifts in the spirit realm are quickened and heightened so that you may achieve God's purpose for your life. God chooses who and how He uses people for His purpose. Your background, social, or economic standing bears no effect on what Yah calls for you to do.

You see, Saul was a man of lowly means. In fact, he didn't live better than many of us and was of a simple mind. He didn't desire to become king, but that didn't change God's plan for his life. The Bible says in *1 Samuel 9:12-13*:

"Am I not a Benjaminite, from the least of the tribes of Israel? And is not my clan the humblest of all the clans of the tribe of Benjamin? Why, then, have you spoken to me in this way?"

This humility is commonly found among new believers when they are engrafted into the body of Christ. Like with King Saul, the Lord has ushered us to His table through a man or woman of God, similar to how Samuel welcomed Saul.

Whatsoever the Lord has appointed and set aside for you to do in your life, no man or demonic force in hell can take it from you. No one can take from the Lord or cancel His plans for you. King Saul was the same. His problem was not what man could take from him but what he would give away. King Saul's life was protected as long as he walked in the calling and decrees of the Lord. His life took a terrible turn when the presence of God left and his kingship with it.

I believe there is a lot a believer can learn from the account of King Saul, King David, and a few others like Eli and his sons, Samson and Delilah, Hosea and Gomer, the Prodigal Son, and more. I want to take you down this road of unpacking key people in the Bible and how the decisions they made–that we also can make, can be "***The Biggest Mistake that Can Cost You Everything***!"

I won't leave you hanging, so you know we are going to round this journey out with the saving grace of Christ. Yah can love you when no one else does, and you can miss the mark that God set before you at the beginning of time, but come to yourself and be a recipient of His mercy and grace. The plans He has for us are great, but we have to accept His will, and these stories exemplify why.

KINGS

KING SAUL THE FALLEN KING

Saul's appointment with destiny could not start without him first proving he could be obedient. "Thou shall obey your mother and father" was God's instruction in the *10 Commandments* handed to Moses for him to share with God's people (*Exodus 20:12*). What we may not realize is following God's commandments set us up for His rewards. To be used by God, we have to understand obedience is greater than sacrifice (*1 Samuel 15:22*). When the Lord gives His orders, it is not up to us to consider if we agree before we obey.

Have you realized that as children, our parents teach us the foundations of life? They help us to set boundaries and teach the simplest things, like how to walk, eat, and when to go to sleep. Sometimes, we learn the importance and master the lessons, and sometimes, we don't realize it until we are much further in life. As a youth, you can probably eat anything you want without gaining a pound. When you get older, you find out unhealthy eating habits will lead to a plethora of problems not seen at the inception.

Likewise, when we are in school, we learn reading, math, science, logic, and other subjects that we don't think we need at the time. As we grow up to be engineers, teachers, or instructors, we learn that those subjects all have intrinsic value. Each precept learned stacks, precept upon precept. We see the building blocks of life take form (*Isaiah 28:10*). No matter what your future holds, your current state will work to help shape your destiny.

Saul passed the first lesson to obey his mother and father. He was faithful and consistent in following instructions with the little he had. Saul was from the tribe of Benjamin, and of all tribes to be born, he was from the smallest, the youngest, and the most humble (*1 Samuel 19:12-13*). In life, we must remain humble and take our lessons with patience. The request Saul's father made of him to go out and track down donkeys may not appear to be the mission of the century. Going on the search for the missing donkeys was a test of Saul's humility and a demonstration of his character.

<u>1 Samuel 9: 3</u>

Now, the donkeys of Kish, Saul's father, were lost. So Kish said to Saul, his son, "Take one of the young men with you, and arise, go and look for the donkeys.

Have you been asked to do something that you felt at the time made no sense? I know as children, we are asked to clean everything, cook, wash walls, and take our siblings everywhere with us. It is tempting to think of yourself as a slave by how you are given tasks. At church, you may start in a humble position as well. Cleaning bathrooms, serving food, volunteering, or doing whatever needs to be done. Service of some kind appears to be demanded to grow in life as well as in the Kingdom of God.

What do we learn from doing these seemingly small tasks? What can a CEO learn from being a person at the bottom? I believe you get the building blocks for a strong foundation. I think it does add to what you understand about the entire business at hand. You also know what it means to start from an entry-level position to better relate to others or find solutions.

King Saul was no different. He had to pay his dues, and that started with searching for donkeys. Of all the animals to be sent out to recover, the Lord had Saul's dad send him out for donkeys. What do donkeys represent? What was their function—purpose, or importance for Saul and his family? Donkeys are creatures that are referenced several times in the Bible. The animal can bear very strong burdens and is considered a reliable helper to man.

This animal is also a symbol of peace, industry, and wealth. Donkeys are the beasts chosen by Yah to demonstrate humility and trust and mark epic moments in life. Abraham used a donkey in *Genesis 22:3* to travel with him and Isaac to where he was supposed to sacrifice his son.

"Abraham got up early in the morning to saddle his donkey, a small act, yet one of obedience to the Lord in order to offer Isaac up to God."

The text would have read very differently by

intent and purpose if Abraham hadn't loaded up a donkey but a horse to go and sacrifice his son. Abraham also didn't pack a bag that he carried on his own shoulders, but he saddled his donkey. A donkey helps men bear heavy burdens and is a helper in a time of need. We learn that Abraham was obedient to the Lord's command, and although his heart may have been heavy for the task, he didn't waiver to be faithful.

Has the Lord asked you to do something that makes you feel heavy? That challenges you to think, is this God or the devil giving me this assignment? How many of us would have assumed it was a bad spirit that would tell us to kill our son? Murder is a sin, and this sin was also listed in the 10 Commandments given to Moses. Surely, God wouldn't want me to kill an innocent man to prove my love for Him, would He?

He didn't require the life of Isaac, but He was testing the faithfulness of Abraham. Sometimes, Yah gives us commands to see if we will follow the instructions. The true reason we may come to learn and possibly will never understand. Sometimes, it is simply because He said so. Why do we expect Yah to give us an account of why He makes certain requests? He is the God of the Universe and of everything living that has died, whether it is human, animal, creature, or spirit.

We would be foolish not to trust Yah, and Abraham was no fool. He trusted the Lord and obeyed His request, and he found the Lord to be faithful. Not only in saving his son's life but for giving him a son to begin with; he and his wife were old when they conceived Isaac.

In *Numbers 22:23-35* the Spirit of God fell on the second animal ever to speak to man, and that animal was a donkey. He enabled the donkey to speak. The donkey did not open his mouth to fight or insult. This animal is not a warring animal but a helper even when he is being wronged.

The donkey saw the angel of the Lord standing in the path with a sword drawn when Balaam didn't. He was sticking his neck out to save the man by redirecting him, like how Christ seeks to save us by redirecting our path from the crooked way to the straight. Balaam, however, was unaware of the animal's desire to help him, so he beat the animal three times for disobeying him. After the third beating, the Lord gave the caring beast speech.

"The donkey said to Balaam. "Am I not your own donkey, which you have always ridden to this day? Have I been in the habit of doing this to you?" "No," he said.

The donkey asked questions to Balaam, and these questions demonstrated his desire to help him. When Balaam's eyes were opened, and he saw the angel with the sword, he then knew he sinned. The donkey wasn't a stumbling block for the man but now a friend. Had the donkey not spoken and stopped in his tracks, the angel said it would have slain Balaam because he was on a reckless path (*Numbers 22:32-33*). Surely, this was the biggest mistake that would have cost him everything, his life!

Another account, and perhaps one of the most profound, was that the Lord Jesus "Yashua," the Christ, also rode on a donkey. Why not a horse? A horse symbolizes war and vengeance, it surely looks more kingly than a measly donkey some would argue. So why a donkey?

He was on a donkey because He had not come here to make war–yet. He came on a special assignment from His Father on High. The donkey symbolizes peace, being a help, a friend, and one who bears strong or heavy burdens for others. Yashua rode through the crowd on a donkey because He was sent to help us.

He was sent to restore peace and communion between man and Yah. Yashua bore a load no other could bear so that man could be restored to the Father, the Creator of All. Jesus will be coming at the Second Coming riding on a horse. This horse does not represent peace and help but war, judgment, vengeance, and vindication.

What else did we learn about the character of Saul? We learned he was committed to a task that demonstrated patience. Patience is a virtuous characteristic, and if you have ever prayed for patience, you will quickly find that the Lord provides you with a test that works patience. Patience comes when you realize your ability to move forward or change course is not within your control. Children are a true way to learn patience.

They have their own mind, and sometimes, our tricks do not work on them. If we are teachers, bosses on our jobs, or lead others at church, that same authority doesn't seem to trickle down to our home, does it? Children seem to be born with the ability to say "no." You ask them to come here, and they say "no." You tell them to eat this or do that, and they say "no." These babies can barely walk and talk, but they will stand on the little power they have and tell you "no." There is power in your words, those spoken and those muted.

We learn patience when our power doesn't improve the situation or hurry it along, but we have to wait and go through it. (I love how Garry Washington writes about Trusting God as We Go Through in his latest book. Check it out.) When babies are newborns, you can yell or encourage them to be quiet, and it won't work sometimes. You can think to spank them for peace or scare them into submission, only to find that also won't work.

They will continue to cry because you don't scare them. They haven't been conditioned to fear you or anything. So, instead of flexing your muscles, you have to learn to comfort them, rock them, sing, make silly faces, and completely change your plans to be about theirs. I took a few naps when I didn't want to because my children did, and after waking up, I was grateful.

We learn patience and are not given it. This relationship reminds me of how Christ also left His home to put down his power, to come here, to be beneath angels to comfort us. Yashua became our manifested help on earth that guides us as our teacher, master, friend, and everything. A loving parent does everything for a baby, and they learn to love them over time.

Children can be stiff-necked and hard to budge, perhaps similar to goats. A baby goat is formerly known as a kid, and this is another adaptation we have made to address children, maybe because children can be just as headstrong as a goat! Goats are separated from sheep, according to the Bible. To follow the father, we need to be more like sheep than goats. Sheep listen to their shepherd and allow themselves to be led by Him; children and people alienated from the shepherd's voice are like goats lost and willing to eat (accept) anything thing.

One of the greatest tools to teach children is through repetition and corrective behaviors. They learn with patience. The same way we learn to be patient with children is a similar example of how the Lord is also patient with us. Yah is the Father of His people, His children.

Have you learned that patience builds character and patience is the tree that gives the fruit of humility? The Lord says we ought to be like children (*Matthew 18:3*) so that we may enter into the Kingdom of God. That simply means we must be teachable; we must be willing to listen and obey God the Father. The reason why Yah commands us to obey our mother and father as children is so that the same commandment as we get older we can apply to Him.

If you never learn to fear your mother and father or reverence and respect them, how can you know how to respect Yah? For that matter, how can we know how to treat others like teachers, elders, police officers, etc? If we don't learn to obey our mother and father, we are not trained to give any respect to someone else. Unruly children walk and run down a reckless path similar to Balaam, and those who choose that path just may find an Angel swinging a sword before them.

Thank the good Lord for the voices that are like the donkey in our lives, warning us to change direction and not to cross roads that could lead to death. Youths are passing away and dropping like flies because they are living reckless lives and not heeding the direction of the Teacher. The ultimate teacher is the Lord, and we must take him seriously—respect Him because He is mighty and Holy.

We shouldn't live recklessly because no man knows the hour when Christ will return or when grace will run out. You don't want to look up and notice that the Spirit of God is gone, and you are walking alone. Remember, no matter where you go in life, stay humble and continue to listen to God because His children never outgrow their Master.

Luke 6:40 says, "We are never above our teacher but are fully trained to be like our teacher." As believers, we are to look like our Father. We are to look like Yahshua/Jesus without trying to replace His presence or Lordship in our lives. Saul later stopped governing himself according to Yah's word with an unreproachable heart of gratitude. He no longer had this child-like faith but attempted to be equal with Yah. He forgot to reverence the Lord as Holy and wiser than himself.

When Saul did not follow orders from our Heavenly Father, as he had learned to follow orders from his earthly father, he made the biggest mistake, which cost him everything. Yah cannot use a person who will not obey Him. Saul didn't question his father on if it were wise to go out in search of the donkeys; he just did it because that was what he was told to do. Yet when the Lord told Him not to take or keep any man alive, he decided to disobey God because he thought he knew better.

Sometimes in life, we are tempted to disobey an order from God, and there are consequences for disobedience. The enemy waits to entrap us with the spirit of compromise. We must remember our humble begins.

The same relationship you start with, Yah, keep that relationship close to your mind, heart, ears, hands, and soul (will and emotions). To know to do good and do it not is sin (*James 4:17*), and sin when it is fully grown leads to death (*James 1:15*). Never forget to remain like a child in the presence of Yah and take every Word from His mouth seriously. Your obedience or lack thereof could cost you to sin unto death (*1 John 5:16*).

Even though Saul did not die instantly after his disobedience, like the prophet Iddo, his relationship with God was dead. King Saul was a walking deadman, and it showed. He had no power, and those close to him knew that the anointing had left him. Rage grew within him against the future king, David, because he was a constant reminder of his fall from grace.

You can operate in your gift but be dead inside, lacking the power, anointing, and Spirit of God. So, how did a man who started on the right path get so far away from Yah? What went wrong, you ask? Let our study continue to *1 Samuel 9:15-17*.

<u>I Samuel 9:15 – 17 KJV</u>

15 Now the LORD had told Samuel in his ear a day before Saul came, saying,

16 Tomorrow about this time I will send thee a man out of the land of Benjamin, and thou shalt anoint him to be captain over my people Israel, that he may save my people out of the hand of the Philistines: for I have looked upon my people because their cry is come unto me.

17 And when Samuel saw Saul, the LORD said unto him, Behold, the man whom I spake to thee of! This same shall reign over my people.

Your calling is always orchestrated at a higher level than you think. The Almighty did not call Saul or look for a king simply because He wanted someone to stand out. He didn't call Saul so he could toot, "I started from the bottom, and now I am here." He called him because he had a great work for him to perform. He called him because His people wanted a king even though they had the King of Kings already.

When Yah has made up His mind to do a thing, He will notify His prophets to initiate that transition on earth. He called Samuel, a faithful man of God, to carry out anointing Saul. Saul did not call himself to be king. Actually, he had no clue. Do you feel that you are called to something but have no clue as to what it is? If a prophet was sent to you with a Word from Yah, would you listen or turn a deaf ear because you couldn't believe the task God called you to?

Do you know how important it is for us to be able to hear the Voice of Yah? His voice is a tone in your ear, a scripture you turn to in your Bible, or an inner knowing that has a clear voice that delivers instructions. No matter your connection, be sure to hear from Yah to be certain of your journey. If your maturity in Him is not certain, pray for wise counsel to affirm His Word in your life.

Many ask the question is Yah pleased with me? The truth is if you are in His will, even if you please no one else, you will be pleasing Him. Your obedience and devotion are what He wants. Samuel was devoted to Yah even as a child. He was the first fruit gift to Yah from his mother, Hannah.

When Samuel got the instruction from God to prepare for a king, He would pick from the tribe of Benjamin. He knew his assignment. God was specific with His instructions to him. For Yah, time is not of the essence. He is the author of time, and no clock dictates His plans but His own sovereignty. I am sure Saul was living his seemingly unimportant regular life, being faithful over little, and the Father determined to give him much more.

Time is more beneficial for man to communicate with because we are not omnipresent or omniscient. We need a way to track and keep up with each other, and time helps us to do that. Can you imagine setting a meeting or making plans without a way to track time? The answer should be "no" because the chances of the meeting happening are slim if you both are not on the same metric for gauging time.

Our number one goal should be for us to have the same timezone as Yah. Hence, His will, plans, and vision for our lives should take precedence over anything else. This might not sound great in the beginning because we all, at one point, thought we knew enough to determine what direction we would take. Only to find that we were wrong and God had the right answer all along.

What I love is that Saul didn't have to pray for Yah to make him King. He never asked to be rich or for more than what he had. In our day and time, people suggest that we should be more ambitious, dream bigger, think larger, and want more, but in Yah's timing, we find none of that matters.

The right next step requires us to get in step with God. To get into step, we must see the value in God's way and choose His way over our own. We are to seek the Kingdom of God and His righteousness so that all things will be added to us (*Matthew*

6:33).

Another truth we must accept is God's timing doesn't consult us for our opinion or approval. God speaks what is final, perfect, truth, and must not be changed. The Lord requires our obedience to His command because the Bible reads, "**You are not a true believer unless you follow His commandments** *(John 14:15).*" In addition, He says that obedience is better than sacrifice, and His sheep know His voice *(John 10:27).*

The Lord gives us all gifts because we are His children, and He prepares us to serve in His kingdom. Spiritual gifts are a heavily visited topic among believers because gifts feed the body. Gifts were given to build up the saints of Yah, and collectively, we are to operate like one body to help lead the unbeliever to Christ. You cannot know your function or be certain you will fulfill your purpose without understanding your gifts. Your purpose and gifts are connected, and they work together.

Although there are tools many use, such as quizzes, tests, and the like, to determine your gifts in 20 to 100 questions, but the best method is asking God. Who best to tell you your gifts than Yah? He knows why He made you, and although you may not have the appearance of your assignment, Yah will take you the rest of the way. There is no caste system in God. His kingdom is not made out of man's traditions but His choosing.

C2

JONATHAN: THE
FAITHFUL
SERVANT

Anyone can see that Jonathan had a heart for Yah. He did what was right in the sight of God, even if it could cost his life. He was not biased toward David nor jealous of his accomplishments. He was a true friend and faithful to his father. He wasn't afraid to be a warrior and travel with the troops. He couldn't be likened to a lazy, spoiled child cooped up in his room playing games, chasing women, and doing things not royal.

He was with his father, supporting the king, and was mighty in battle. This same loyalty he brought to his relationship and friendship with David. The Bible says, "My command is this: **Love each other as I have loved you. Greater love has no one than this: to lay down one's life for one's friends**" *(John 15:12-13)*.

In *1 Samuel 20*, Jonathan risks his life to seek out a matter for his friend. He was willing to face the unknown that David knew could be bad for him to help his friend. A javelin intended for King David, was tossed at him by his own father because he knew Jonathan was loyal to a king greater than he.

I Samuel 20:30-34 KJV

33 And Saul cast a javelin at him to smite him: whereby Jonathan knew that it was determined of his father to slay David.

34 So Jonathan arose from the table in fierce anger and did eat no meat the second day of the month: for he was grieved for David, because his father had done him shame.

Some people mock when you see children being defiant to their parents. Children who turn their back on racism to do what thus says Yah. We laughed and mocked Harry for leaving the palace and, as far as we know, to follow after God. How strong does one have to be to stand against a kingdom? A prayer for strength and blessings for those who turn their backs on their own family, specifically their parents, to obey Yah.

30 Then Saul's anger was kindled against Jonathan, and he said unto him, Thou son of the perverse rebellious woman, do not I know that thou hast chosen the son of Jesse to thine own confusion, and unto the confusion of thy mother's nakedness?

31 For as long as the son of Jesse liveth upon the ground, thou shalt not be established, nor thy kingdom. Wherefore now send and fetch him unto me, for he shall surely die.

Do you know why people hate? Why do people kill off the strong and try their best to stop the hand of Yah? Saul didn't want to lose the kingship. He didn't want the change of tide. He didn't want to stand with Yah and His choice. He decided to fight a losing battle with javelins, spears, and the measly weapons he had in his possession.

BUT no poisons or no deadly weapons can stop the plans of Yah for His children. No witch or warlock can resurrect a different outcome contrary to the Word of God. King Saul got so desperate to hold on to his kingly anointing and pass it to his son that he thought to murder David. He sought a witch in hopes she would say something different than what he already knew: King David would be the next king.

If He says "Yes," who can tell Him "no?" Who can say the blessing on King David can't be so? Who can tell Yah to pick a new people because they demand it? People think they can kill everything that scares them or kill what makes them feel inferior. Only Pharoah found that the more you try to stump out God's anointed, the more they multiply! The more he tried to silence David's name, the more he heard it.

When Jonathan gave David the warning and embraced him as a friend, David always knew what would befall him because of the side he chose. Have you ever met people who knew speaking up for others would cost them their lives? Martin Luther King knew speaking up for the black community and unifying people would cost him his life. Stephen Darby knew preaching truth would cost him his. The

Seven Sons in *2 Maccabees* knew not eating pork (honoring Yah) would cost them their lives, but they laid it down righteously.

What are you willing to sacrifice out of faithfulness and righteousness? Yashua gave His life faithfully on the cross to redeem man. Can you do what is right if it means it costs you your life, your comfort, your position, and your possessions? David wept more when he embraced Jonathan because he knew the weight of the promise and covenant they both made before Yah.

<u>1 Samuel 20:8-17 KJV</u>

8 Therefore thou shalt deal kindly with thy servant; for thou hast brought thy servant into a covenant of the Lord with thee: notwithstanding, if there be in me iniquity, slay me thyself; for why shouldest thou bring me to thy father?

9 And Jonathan said, Far be it from thee: for if I knew certainly that evil were determined by my father to come upon thee, then would not I tell it thee?

10 Then said David to Jonathan, Who shall tell me? or what if thy father answer thee roughly?

11 And Jonathan said unto David, Come, and let us go out into the field. And they went out both of them into the field.

12 And Jonathan said unto David, O Lord God of Israel, when I have sounded my father about to morrow any time, or the third day, and, behold, if there be good toward David, and I then send not unto thee, and shew it thee;

13 The Lord do so and much more to Jonathan: but if it please my father to do thee evil, then I will shew it thee, and send thee away, that thou mayest go in peace: and the Lord be with thee, as he hath been with my father.

14 And thou shalt not only while yet I live shew me the kindness of the Lord, that I die not:

15 But also thou shalt not cut off thy kindness from my house for ever: no, not when the Lord hath cut off the enemies of David every one from the face of the earth.

16 So Jonathan made a covenant with the house of David, saying, Let the Lord even require it at the hand of David's enemies.

17 And Jonathan caused David to swear again, because he loved him: for he loved him as he loved his own soul.

This covenant was not just a plea of friendship; it was David's commitment not to deal wrongfully with Jonathan's house for as long as he lived. It was Jonathan being like Rahab and helping the spies enter the promised land. Jonathan knew he was not the crown prince. He told David the truth when he could have lied. David knew the position Jonathan was in and the faithfulness of Yah to save him alive by using King Saul's son to be his informant.

1 Samuel 20:41-42 KJV

41 And as soon as the lad was gone, David arose out of a place toward the south, and fell on his face to the ground, and bowed himself three times: and they kissed one another, and wept one with another, until David exceeded.

42 And Jonathan said to David, Go in peace, forasmuch as we have sworn both of us in the name of the Lord, saying, The Lord be between me and thee, and between my seed and thy seed forever. And he arose and departed: and Jonathan went into the city.

Not only did this great friend help him this time, but during battle, when King David's heart started to wain, who came through for him again? It was Jonathan.

1 Samuel 23:16-18 KJV

16 And Jonathan Saul's son arose and went to David into the wood, and strengthened his hand in God.

17 And he said unto him, Fear not: for the hand of Saul my father shall not find thee; and thou shalt be king over Israel, and I shall be next unto thee; and that also Saul my father knoweth.

18 And they two made a covenant before the Lord: and David abode in the woods, and Jonathan went to his house.

Don't we all need a voice or helping hand to

be outstretched to pull us out of our sunken place? Jonathan was that friend. He wouldn't let King David's spirit fall, no matter what it looked like. Seeing Jonathan support Yah's will, I am sure, brought him comfort. Some people in our lives are down for us and will help us genuinely. When you find a friend like this, they are your brother or your sister, no matter your race, country of origin, or current location.

When Jonathan came to encourage David, the covenant they made was for Jonathan to serve David as King and be his second. How many in this position would bow their head to a man who has not yet obtained the crown? How many would go against their natural father for the service of their heavenly Father? How tempting it must have been to listen to the voices telling him he should be king and not King David!

He had to overcome where his father failed. He was able to silence the voices of the people and the devil all the same. Have you found yourself wrestling within yourself and everyone outside of you to do the will of the Father?

Although David knew someday he would be king, he was not going to push the manifestation of his promise ahead of Yah's timing. King David knew he had to remain submitted to Yah to obtain what was promised to him by God. In our lives, do you have a vision, a promise from Yah? If so, I want to encourage you that whatever God has promised will come to pass.

Isaiah records in *55:11* that whatever Yah

sends His Word out to do, it will accomplish it. Heaven and earth can pass away before His Word fails. Remain confident and keep your hands clean of any blood. This also means keeping your lips clean of saying things out of spite, gossiping, or wishing for someone's death. We are to be honest, bring truth, and be peacekeepers (*Matthew 5:9*).

2 Samuel 1:5-12 KJV

5 And David said unto the young man that told him, How knowest thou that Saul and Jonathan his son be dead?

6 And the young man that told him said, As I happened by chance upon mount Gilboa, behold, Saul leaned upon his spear; and, lo, the chariots and horsemen followed hard after him.

7 And when he looked behind him, he saw me and called unto me. And I answered, Here am I.

8 And he said unto me, Who art thou? And I answered him, I am an Amalekite.

9 He said unto me again, Stand, I pray thee, upon me, and slay me: for anguish is come upon me because my life is yet whole in me.

10 So I stood upon him, and slew him, because I was sure that he could not live after that he was fallen: and I took the crown that was upon his head, and the bracelet that was on his arm, and have brought them hither unto my lord.

11 Then David took hold of his clothes, and rent

them; and likewise all the men that were with him:

12 And they mourned, and wept, and fasted until even, for Saul, and for Jonathan his son, and for the people of the Lord, and for the house of Israel; because they were fallen by the sword.

King David mourned over the lives of both Jonathan and King Saul. He knew a great friend to him had died, and so have other men and women of Yah in that same battle. He was not pleased with the report. War under these circumstances doesn't make a righteous man happy.

War should make men reflect on what is important. It is said when a nation fights among itself and, people are lost during the shuffle. Church splits should hurt us, division in the body should hurt us, and seeing Yah's people dying in a battle they should have won hurt King David.

Hearing a man take the life of the king with no care of the implications was a gross error and the Biggest mistake this Amalikite could have made. He died the same, and the covenant that David made to Jonathan he was determined to keep. He not only honored the deaths of both King Saul and Jonathan, but he also regarded his covenant with Jonathan through how he treated Mephibosheth. He gave him a seat at the table and never debased his importance.

Even though King Saul was called to be king, his son was not. Now, the risk we take when we leave God out of the process of searching for our purpose and gifts is that we may be malfunctioning in the body. Can you imagine seeing a body haphazardly put together? Your hands are the feet, the arms are the legs, the head is pointing in the wrong direction, and the list goes on and on. What can the body accomplish if people are not in right position to be the hands and feet of Yah? The body functions as a plague or cancerous cell if we are not operating to represent the Kingdom of God on earth.

In *1 Corinthians 12*, we learn that gifts from the Lord include wisdom, knowledge, faith, healing, miracles, prophecy, distinguishing between spirits (discernment), tongues, and the interpretation of tongues (*1 Corinthians 12:7-10)*. All these are empowered by the Spirit of Yah, who apportions to each individually as He wills (*1 Corinthians 12:11*). The Lord has a plan for your life, and your gift is an asset for getting you in the right position to win.

In Ephesians 4:11, the spiritual gifts that makeup what is commonly referred to as the "five-fold ministry" are given. The "five-fold ministry" is made up of apostles, prophets, evangelists, preachers, and teachers. These gifts are bestowed upon God's children for the edification of the body of Christ. Gifts are not given for man to decide how to be used but for the Lord's instruction.

Let's revisit the parable that paints the best picture of spiritual gifts briefly (*Matthew 25:14-30*). God gave three people gifts, which were reflected in talents or shekels. The three varied in what they did with their talents. The two that did the will of the

Lord and returned a harvest used their talent for the edification of the Kingdom, and they got a greater reward. The foolish man, who buried the talent and returned nothing on top of what he was given, was called a lazy, wicked servant and cast out the gates.

Choosing to use your talent for God and not bury the gifts is the ideal posture. In the case of Saul, instructions were very much needed as he didn't appear to be qualified to be the King of the Hebrew nation; in fact, no man is qualified without Yah to lead even themselves. For him to have a fighting chance to lead, he had to seek the Lord every step of the way because there was no king before him. There was something about Saul that the Lord liked that made Him choose Saul to become king.

One of Saul's gifts was leadership, and two other gifts he had were wisdom and knowledge. These gifts were birthed in him long before he realized but they needed to be cultivated. The first lesson any good leader ought to learn or possess is a teachable spirit. Before anyone can lead, they must first know how to follow. Saul had to hear the voice of the Lord and follow the commands of God because he had to lay the foundation for Yah's people.

Saul had already proved in his youth that he was capable and raised to listen and follow the voice of his father. The foundation was there for him to listen to his heavenly Father's Voice. If we don't pass the first step, it will likely impede our ability to follow the next step. Saul's next step was to learn the path of God and, after learning to lead by example.

He had to spend lots of time with Yah and God's appointed people to develop and mature the talents He put in him. By developing your gifts, the Lord can call you into the game.

Can you imagine a star player that has never had a coach? Could he have great raw talent? A thousand times, the answer is "yes." However, can that same talented person see his weaknesses? Do they innately know how to fix the problems they have with their stance, swing, or other movements?

Can you imagine any great player in any field not having a coach to show them how to do a thing better? Raw talent can put you in view, but developed talent will keep you at the top. A raw cashew can kill you, but a refined nut can nourish your body. The more you develop your gifts, the more your name will be called. If you work at a job, are you going to call a newbie to get something done you value?

Would it be wise to bank your business on a person that has no training? It could be a shot in the dark that, during this meeting, the person lands the deal, but is that bankable, or is it beginner luck? As students, we quickly learn that we don't know everything. If we choose not to hide from our help but consult them, we will always grow. Having a teachable spirit always includes being honest about where you are.

Can you imagine a child void of the foundation to obey their parents and never allow anyone to shape them? These children are preyed upon and picked out by the time they are in 3rd grade to support the prison system. The system writes off children who lack the ability to follow the rules as the future of the prison industrial complex.

The rules I am talking about are not the conditioning that happens in school. Conditioning children not to question school education is not what I mean. To learn, you must question and consider the information you are presented with. Not everything we are taught is for our benefit. Some things are intended to hold us in a mindset contrary to Yah's design.

These traditions should be broken and not supported. Yet, to understand what is the enemy of your faith, future, and purpose, you often need to understand your opposition. No sport would exist without offense and defense or two opposing sides. To take down a system, you will likely have to go inside.

To change your habits, you have to go inside your thought patterns. To change laws, you will likely have to go into politics. To change a community, you have to be part of the community. To win a war, you have to enter the battle.

Saul did not tell God to choose him to play this game; in fact, he tried to talk Samuel and God out of it. He had more excuses for why he shouldn't be king than to be king. Have you ever tried to talk yourself out of things God intended for you? But God! Telling Him you are weak and choosing to be putty in His hands makes you a tool He can use.

God saw this virtue in Saul when He chose him. God chooses us, and if we want Him to draw near to us, we must first draw near to Him (*James 4:8*). We get close so that we may hear and acknowledge Him in our hearts. Something of note is that when God gives us gifts, He anoints them so we can serve.

Saul had no possible way of growing to be king in the natural. He was from the youngest tribe, with the lowest hierarchy and the smallest tribe in number. All the way around, he would appear to be the wrong candidate for the job. If there had been a vote by the people with our standards, he would have also failed because his money was not long enough to win a campaign. The king's anointing that God gave him put him in a position he could never earn. Yes, the presence of the Lord, His anointing married to our gift(s), will make the impossible possible.

<u>I Samuel 14:47 – 48 KJV</u>

47 So Saul took the kingdom over Israel, and fought against all his enemies on every side, against Moab, and against the children of Ammon, and against Edom, and against the kings of Zobah, and against the Philistines: and whithersoever he turned himself, he vexed them.

48 And he gathered a host, and smote the Amalekites, and delivered Israel out of the hands of them that spoiled them.

Making the bold statement that God opens the door for you that cannot be shut should have a reference point. *Deuteronomy 28:9-11* the Lord says, "**We are blessed in the city and blessed in the field**;" furthermore, He says He will make us to "prosper" and "abound" in everything we do. This same truth is supported by *1 Samuel 14:47-48* when the Bible states having the Presence of God as you carry out divine assignments that the final result is victory.

When we walk with the Spirit of Yah, it is equivalent to walking with the Ark of the Covenant. The presence of Yah has to be with you at all times for the victory to be yours and for Him to fight your battles. When the Lord fights your battles, it may not make sense or look achievable to the natural eye, but the spiritual eye sees you winning.

Saul was able to defeat the Moabites, Ammonites, Edomites, etc., not because he was the King of Israel but because the Presence of Yah was with him. A grave mistake Saul would make was to believe the power and influence he had was his own. His influence was borrowed. Like how *Deuteronomy 28* listed blessings in obedience, it also listed curses for those who didn't do what the Lord said.

Somehow, Saul lost his way as a child of God, which is a requirement to stay in Yah's will for your life. It should bring great comfort to know that we don't have to be strong warriors or the best at anything for the Lord to bless us. He says to us that in our weakness He is made strong, so take courage if you don't feel you are the best or you lack the resources to excel; that will not stop the plans God has for you (*2 Corinthians 12:9-10*)!

Don't let adversity make you believe God is not in your life. During our battles, the Lord can be glorified because He makes us triumphant over our problems, situations, and our enemies. Challenges will come to us all. Saul had battle after battle that he had to fight, and God gave him victory. That same God can give you victory in any facet of your life, and surely, where He commanded you to go, He can pave the way. Keep the Presence of Yah in your life and conform your lifestyle to a victorious one. Where the Spirit of the Lord is, our battles will always be won, and the favor of the Lord will be on our lives.

I Samuel 15:7 – 9 KJV

7 And Saul smote the Amalekites from Havilah until thou comest to Shur, that is over against Egypt.

8 And he took Agag the king of the Amalekites alive, and utterly destroyed all the people with the edge of the sword.

9 But Saul and the people spared Agag, and the best of the sheep, and of the oxen, and of the fatlings, and the lambs, and all that was good, and would not utterly destroy them: but every thing that was vile and refuse, that they destroyed utterly.

Saul fed into compromise and tried to rationalize the Word God gave him for his benefit—don't do this. Don't try to bend the Truth to fit your lifestyle, your desire, your ministry platform, or anything else. When Saul changed his instructions, he implied there was an error in the instructions, which was an egregious mistake Saul made. The Bible instructs us not to add nor take away from the Word of God (*Revelation 22:18-20*). When we change and alter Yah's Word to fit our own liking, we have accepted another gospel with new instructions, and it is as Paul asked, "Who has bewitched you (*Galatians 3:1*)?"

The Lord specifically told him to destroy everything that the Amalekites had in their possession and not leave a thing of theirs. King Saul, however, only destroyed some of their things and killed most of the people but took many things he felt were good in his sight. He took animals and spared the life of their king.

Have you ever noticed how we take the gifts Yah has given us and use them for our own benefit? I don't dare say to use them for the devil's devices, but we do that too, don't we? Yah can gift some to sing, dance, talk, write, act, cook, and so forth. Instead of using our gifts to bless the righteous name of Yah, we allow compromise to enter.

Instead of remaining humble as we make it through the ranks, we start to believe we own the talent we have. That is "I" got me here and not Yah. We believe, even for a moment, that we don't need God, and we can take it from here. What makes us so pompous to think we have outgrown Yah and His teachings? That His covering is no longer necessary because we have friends, money, a husband, status, or things that say I am stable in my possessions and position.

Only this God made a king chew the cud for 7 years! His nails grew out, his hair, he looked like a wild animal before he came to his senses. Nebuchadnezzar was a king that everyone knew the Father had touched His mind. He took his authority and debased him down to an animal to prove that no one is too high to be touched by Yah (*Daniel 4:25-35*)!

Why did Saul feel comfortable changing God's plans, and also why do we? Next, why did he believe there would be no consequence for his disobedience? What because he was king–the king that Yah made? People will talk our heads up and make us believe our natural titles make us able to fight against Yah.

Have you met people who believe they are God? They think because they have money and status, they can rule, create, and make others obey them. They lean on these physical things to justify manipulating spiritual matters for others. They use laws to change what you believe and how you think spiritually. They believe their system is equal to God's system, and they try to use His words to their benefit by saying, "obey the rules of the land."

Saul did not follow the command of the Lord but rested his confidence in man. Saul is without any excuse because he could hear the Voice of the Lord directly. He had the presence of Yah operating in his life to an undeniable degree, and yet he thought he could lie and hide like Adam and Eve when they sinned.

We will not be able to sweet talk Yah or conceal our true hearts' desire and intent, nor defend our actions with lies. God is omnipresent and omnipotent, and He knows all, especially the hearts and desires of His children (*Jeremiah 1:5*).

You can see clearly that anytime one goes wrong or disobeys God's command, it's very difficult for that person to come back to God. The reason it is so hard is because from the bottom of your heart, when you sinned, you knew the presence of Yah was over your life. Saul was supposed to go and report to Samuel, but Samuel didn't hear from Saul and had to go and confront him.

When Samuel confronted Saul, he made it as if everything was fine. When Samuel made bare the things that were thought to be secret, Saul confessed and lied and said it was for Yah. How can we sin against God and then say we sinned for God? Fresh and salt water cannot come out of the same vessel, nor can disobedience be supported by the notion "I sinned to please God;" it is an oxymoron (*James 3:11*).

I believe the prophet Samuel was there not only to rebuke King Saul for his disobedience to the Lord but also to extend an opportunity for him to get in right step with Yah. Saul was given a chance to admit, fess up, and repent for his actions, but instead, he blamed others. When the Lord was walking in the garden in the cool of the day, He approached Adam and Eve for their transgressions, who also blamed each other and the serpent (*Genesis 3:8-13*).

This did not stop God's judgment. For one, they lied to Yah's face, then tried to explain why lying was okay. Not a good idea. Saul didn't realize at the time it was a privilege to acknowledge his sin and repent. Yah desired to forgive him because sin caused a separation between Yah and us (*Isaiah 59:2-3*).

Christians and non-believers can fall into this trap, whereby we blame others for our situation. Stop blaming people and acknowledge any shortcomings of obedience in your life while God is still here for you. Keep your allegiance to Yah.

1 Samuel 28:7 KJV

7 Then said Saul unto his servants, Seek me a woman that hath a familiar spirit, that I may go to her, and enquire of her. And his servants said to him, Behold, there is a woman that hath a familiar spirit at Endor.

Saul gave in to seducing spirits, and because the Lord rejected his prayers, he turned to divination. Fear made him reach his lowest of low. He went to a psyche to help him discern the future because the unknown eluded and scared him. He allowed fear to scare him to death. Spiritually, he was dead, and his flesh was not too far behind.

If your life is in God's hands, you need not worry if you don't hear His voice. The confidence of the believer is to know that the Lord cares for you.

When the Lord removes His hand, desperation may tempt you to seek the devil for help. This, too, only increases the wedge between you and Yah.

This verse also points to Saul's true heart, which was filled with fear. Saul sought out a woman of divination and asked her to resurrect the man of God, Samuel. He woke Samuel from his rest to ask him to plead to Yah on his behalf; that, too, failed. Samuel could not reverse what Yah had already spoken concerning him. He was simply too late, and his biggest mistake, lying to Yah, could not be reversed. When Saul thought he was ready to repent, God was not interested in listening. The time had passed him by. Yes, it is possible to miss your chance at redemption.

Forgiveness is a process between the receiver and the giver. If one does not participate, forgiveness is a challenge and impossible with Yah. Forgiveness is done to please God and has very little to do with man initially. By offering and receiving forgiveness, we help each other, but the core is to please God.

Saul grieved the Holy Spirit with his actions, reaction to his sin, and continued steps to please his own agenda. God wants us to remember our first love. He desires that we always put His thoughts, desires, and plans as our priority. It is only what God thinks and says that should dictate our life decisions. Saul started his journey with Yah by obeying His Word, principles, and Voice.

He grew to believe that perhaps he deserved the position, the title, and the office of king. He had fought battles and won. He fit the physical physique of a king, and the people loved him. He forgot, however, that before the Lord came and built him up, he was working a regular job. He came from the smallest tribe. He was not born of promise, but God said something different and called him blessed.

God chose Saul, and King Saul returned the favor by disowning Him. He believed in the hype and disobeyed Yah. He exchanged the thoughts of God for the thoughts of others. He put man before Yah.

Saul's end was wallowing in fear. Fear ate him from the inside out, and every move he made was out of terror. The power he thought he had faded. The fame he had with the people was drowned out by David killing tens of thousands. The people stopped singing his praises and those of David instead. His children sided with the future king, and the prophet that called him had now called David.

Saul had lost it all. He lost his relationship with God, his office, and the kingdom. His children weren't on his side either. Saul lost it all when he separated from Yah. Our lives can be the same as King Saul, going in a downward cycle that will end with us having nothing. No peace, hope, and fear will rest in our hearts and minds.

Don't allow fear, doubt, and pride to separate you from the Love of Yah. If there is sin that barricades your prayers from reaching heaven, renounce your sin, praying in spirit and in truth. The only way to move God is to follow His way. To please God, we must pray in spirit and in truth (*John 4:24*).

SONS

C3

ELI'S LOST
BATTLE:
THE DEATH OF
HIS LEGACY

Samuel was called as a young man to serve the Lord, but before he became the prophet we know, he did tasks like sweeping the floors, I am sure doing the dishes, and the like to serve Eli around the temple. When God first called his name, and he answered, he was not ready to be fully used by God because he wasn't mature in his gifting yet. Samuel had to allow Eli to teach him how to develop his raw talent.

The truth, Samuel was a miracle child. His mother was barren for many years, and she prayed aplenty to have Samuel. She was so sincere about having a son that she promised Yah that if He gave her a son, she would give that son back to Him.

1 Samuel 1:11 KJV

11 And she vowed a vow and said, *"O Lord of hosts, if you will indeed look on the affliction of your servant and remember me and not forget your servant, but will give to your servant a son, then I will give him to the Lord all the days of his life, and no razor shall touch his head."*

Hannah was so sincere in prayer that Eli, who

watched her, thought she was drunk. He came to her to tell her to put her drink away from her and not to disrespect the place of Yah. Amazing how some people have strong convictions against you but can falter when the same people who need a rebuke are their own children. They can see your sins, problems, and issues but cannot see those from the ones they love.

<u>1 Samuel 1:12-16 ESV</u>

12 As she continued praying before the Lord, Eli observed her mouth.

13 Hannah was speaking in her heart; only her lips moved, and her voice was not heard. Therefore, Eli took her to be a drunken woman.

14 And Eli said to her, "How long will you go on being drunk? Put your wine away from you."

15 But Hannah answered, "No, my lord, I am a woman troubled in spirit. I have drunk neither wine nor strong drink, but I have been pouring out my soul before the Lord.

16 Do not regard your servant as a worthless woman, for all along I have been speaking out of my great anxiety and vexation."

Have you ever been so heavy about something you needed and wanted from God that you didn't care what it looked like to other people? Have you been so desperate to get a prayer through that you cried all night long? You stayed up watching every sermon, writing down scriptures to play on repeat, and you repetitively came to God to speak to Him about your needs.

To be a woman married to a great man who had a second wife who was contributing to the family by bearing children, and you are the first wife with none, felt shameful. Hannah wanted to stop being provoked and made fun of, but she also wanted to be a part of something bigger than herself. She wanted to give back to Yah, her husband, and her legacy. She wanted to matter and feel worthy of the love she was given.

Perhaps you, too, are wanting to feel deserving of your love? But maybe Yah closed her womb to show her something about herself. The love of God is something we don't deserve, but by His mercy, He gives it. Not because of what we can do for Him but because there is something he wants to display within us. Hannah had to learn, like us, everything we want, we may not get in our timing, but Yah is never late. You can still be loved if you don't bear children. Women are more than baby-making machines. She was loved more by her husband than by the second wife despite her lack of bearing children.

<u>1 Samuel 1:4-8 ESV</u>

4 On the day when Elkanah sacrificed, he would give portions to Peninnah, his wife, and to all her sons and daughters.

5 But to Hannah he gave a double portion, because he loved her, though the Lord had closed her womb.[a]

6 And her rival used to provoke her grievously

to irritate her because the Lord had closed her womb.

7 So it went on year by year. As often as she went up to the house of the Lord, she used to provoke her. Therefore, Hannah wept and would not eat.

8 And Elkanah, her husband, said to her, "Hannah, why do you weep? And why do you not eat? And why is your heart sad? Am I not more to you than ten sons?"

At times, the love of another person cannot overshadow the pain we feel because we may be void of what we prayed for. If we have debased our value because we have listened to other people, it only takes Yah to dig us out of this great depression. Yes, He can use people to give us His Word, but it is His Word that has set our minds and hearts at peace.

So, if you are praying for something that appears to tarry, drag along, or doesn't appear to be coming through, sometimes we have to bombard heaven and ask for others to pray with us. Sometimes, you may need an Eli who can come and give you a word.

1 Samuel 1:17-18 ESV

17 Then Eli answered, "Go in peace, and the God of Israel grant your petition that you have made to him."

18 And she said, "Let your servant find favor in your eyes." Then the woman went her way and ate, and her face was no longer sad.

Sometimes you need to get encouraging words from your husband or wife when you are down. So be open to how the Father will lead. We know not everyone will have the same outcome as Hannah and have children. Don't let anything make you believe you are not loved by God because you don't measure up to a social standard.

Do you remember what it felt like when you got what you prayed for? She got the blessed assurance that Yah was coming through for her, so what now? You've been praying for a car, a house, a spouse, a business, children, or a legacy, but what happens when you get it? I love Hannah's prayer, and may it encourage you too. She says:

1 Samuel 2:1-10 NKJV

1

"My heart exults in the Lord;

my horn is exalted in the Lord.

My mouth derides my enemies,

because I rejoice in your salvation.

2

"There is none holy like the Lord:

for there is none besides you;

there is no rock like our God.

3

Talk no more so very proudly,

>let not arrogance come from your mouth;

for the Lord is a God of knowledge,

>and by him actions are weighed.

4

The bows of the mighty are broken,

>but the feeble bind on strength.

5

Those who were full have hired themselves out for bread,

>but those who were hungry have ceased to hunger.

The barren has borne seven,

>but she who has many children is forlorn.

6

The Lord kills and brings to life;

>he brings down to Sheol and raises up.

7

The Lord makes poor and makes rich;

he brings low and he exalts.

8

He raises up the poor from the dust;

> he lifts the needy from the ash heap

to make them sit with princes

> and inherit a seat of honor.

For the pillars of the earth are the Lord's,

> and on them he has set the world.

9

"He will guard the feet of his faithful ones,

> but the wicked shall be cut off in darkness,
>
> for not by might shall a man prevail.

10

The adversaries of the Lord shall be broken to pieces;

> against them he will thunder in heaven.

The Lord will judge the ends of the earth;

> he will give strength to his king
>
> and exalt the horn of his anointed."

We serve a God who is a mighty judge. He looks on the weak and the strong, governing those in want and in plenty. He looks upon man's heart, and His judgments are perfect. If you are on the right side of God, how comforting is His Word of promise and judgment? But to be in the hands of an angry God when you are the enemy, how scary is that position (*Hebrews 10:31*)?

He says a wicked servant will vow a thing and not deliver (*Ecclesiastes 5:5*). It is better not to vow and do it than to vow and not. Two people were killed in the New Testament because they made a promise to God that they carelessly errored to follow. They lied about the money they received and promised to donate to Yah. They hoped to hide their shame, but only they grieved Yah, so He put them both to sleep.

Again, were you, like Hannah, faithful to do what you said you would, or were you all lip service and no action, all bark and no bite? If you have wronged your brother, the Bible says to go and make peace before you lift your petition to heaven in prayer (*Matthew 5:24*). How much more do we need to go and make amends with Yah if we have offended Him? It can make us loathe ourselves when we fall short of the standard, the glory of God, can't it? Rightfully so, it can make us scared when we have taken Yah's love for us for granted.

I am sure Eli struggled with His love for God and the love he had for His sons. Perhaps he was not like Abraham and would not have sacrificed his sons for Yah, and maybe that was why that wasn't his test. The Father knows what you can handle, what you should be able to do, and what you would likely do. He doesn't set traps to make us fail but to reveal our hearts and assure us we are worth something in His sight. It feels so good when you get something right for the Lord, doesn't it? How depressing it would be to measure your relationship with Yah strictly on your faithfulness and disregard your intentions.

Unlike Hannah, Eli struggled to give his children to Yah. In that, he was not faithful in following Yah's commands and warnings concerning them. He may have had the heart to give back to God, but somewhere, he was compromised.

<u>1 Samuel 2:12-17 ESV</u>

12 Now the sons of Eli were worthless men. They did not know the Lord.

13 The custom of the priests with the people was that when any man offered sacrifice, the priest's servant would come, while the meat was boiling, with a three-pronged fork in his hand,

14 and he would thrust it into the pan or kettle or cauldron or pot. All that the fork brought up the priest would take for himself. This is what they did at Shiloh to all the Israelites who came there.

15 Moreover, before the fat was burned, the priest's servant would come and say to the man who was sacrificing, "Give meat for the priest to roast, for he will not accept boiled meat from you but only raw."

16 And if the man said to him, "Let them burn

the fat first, and then take as much as you wish," he would say, "No, you must give it now, and if not, I will take it by force."

17 Thus the sin of the young men was very great in the sight of the Lord, for the men treated the offering of the Lord with contempt.

Is it possible for us to serve Yah and bring forth children who do not regard Him at all? How is it possible that everyone knew the way of God and how the sacrifice was to be conducted, but Eli's sons were unlearned? Most importantly, if they were not learned, why did he allow them to serve Yah? Some people feel that because they are pastors, their sons or daughters should also minister, even though they know they are wicked children with hearts set apart from God.

It is not worth saving face by allowing your sons or daughters to serve when you know their life is completely contrary to the command of Yah. His sons not only did wrong by the sacrifices, but they also slept with women at the gates. They were disrespecting the holy things of God and still serving as if their sins were of no effect. Not only did Eli assume the people should overlook their sins, but Yah would also.

Sometimes, when we are overcome with grief and feel bad about the behaviors we permit, we submit a broken petition to them with no real consequence. Have you ever seen managers tell their children a command, and nothing happens when they break it? They can be late a million times, they don't work when they show up, and they only come literally for a check. These children are a drag to their families and can mean the downfall of their legacy if their behaviors are not corrected.

Their behaviors are not only bad for the family, but they are also frustrating to the other employees. This resentment can also be picked up by customers and the Almighty Yah sees all. He commands decency and order to be the rule for His children (*1 Corinthians 14:40*). How you live and how you serve does matter to Him, especially if you are in the House of Yah doing these things.

1 Samuel 2:22-25 ESV

22 Now Eli was very old, and he kept hearing all that his sons were doing to all Israel and how they lay with the women who were serving at the entrance to the tent of meeting.

23 And he said to them, "Why do you do such things? For I hear of your evil dealings from all these people.

24 No, my sons; it is no good report that I hear the people of the Lord spreading abroad.

25 If someone sins against a man, God will mediate for him, but if someone sins against the Lord, who can intercede for him?" But they would not listen to the voice of their father, for it was the will of the Lord to put them to death.

Something equally of note is why Eli waited until he was old to check his sons' behavior. Do you know the parents that give their children free rein to raise themselves? I remember being a Sunday school teacher for a 2-year-old and a 4-year-old class. Some children, you could tell, had no discipline at home. Instead of the parents taking ownership of how they are raising their children, they respond by telling the children to act better when they in fact, act the same way at home.

We must train up a child in the right way they ought to go so when they are older, they won't depart from that standard (*Proverbs 22:6*). It's unbelievable that we live in a day and age where the world wants to raise our children so contrary to Biblical principles. Nature used to weigh heavily on how children were brought up, but now, human nature is becoming an optional viewpoint and no longer a fact of science or Biblical teaching.

Raising worldly children is different from raising Kingdom children. Yah's children have standards they must maintain. God will not be void of a witness in this land; He will always keep a remnant that knows His truths (*Romans 11:26*).

What's equally scary is when the Father determines to judge you, and no one can overturn His decision but Him. Everybody's mercy is not the same, and some of us will see our children and loved ones put to death not by the devil but by Yah. I know we think only the devil takes away, but I assure you, the Father is over life and death. Yashua took the keys of death, so who is in control over when someone lives or dies (*Revelation 1:18*)?

Do you believe it is the devil, the world, governments, people, beasts, aliens, or fallen angels? If some people had their way, Yah's people would have been wiped out several times over, but they are still here because when the enemy comes in like a flood, Yah will raise a standard (*Isaiah 59:19*). The same redeeming arm that took His people out of Egypt is still delivering His people even with them not knowing. How good He is that His Son died for those who knew and didn't know Him. Those who will choose to accept or reject Him. The blood can cover all, but it only works for Yah's children, meaning those who take Him as their Lord and Savior.

There is no place you can hide when the God Almighty determines to kill you. Everywhere you run, you will find Him because He is not bound to a border, a life timeline, a blood oath you made, or an agreement you made with the devil. Eli's choice to delay his judgment infuriated Yah. Have you ever let a problem slide for so long that you try to make it okay?

Eli, I am sure, battled to find the best way to talk to his sons. He pushed it off until his old age, perhaps wanting them to change so they could raise the next generation of priests to be better. I am sure he was thinking of his legacy. He perhaps hoped that the next generation would be better than the current. Eli was cursed by God and knew it, but some people are cursed and don't even know it.

Not only did Eli's biggest mistake cost him a legacy in the priesthood, but it also cost his entire family's bloodline to be wiped out! His sons' biggest mistake was to take God for a fool. Their blatant disrespect cost them their lives and the lives of their children.

As a custom, Yah sent a faithful man of God who was able to prophesy to Eli. This man had no name, but he was mentioned in the Bible like the lady who gave to mites that will never be forgotten (*Luke 21:1-4*). Some of you will be sent to people with big churches, big buildings, big houses, long names, and historical presidents. You will give them a message similar to what this man of God gave to Eli. Don't be afraid of how the Lord wants to use you. Out of the mouths of babes, Yah can speak (*Psalms 8:2*)!

1 Samuel 2:27-36 KJV

27 And there came a man of God to Eli and said to him, "Thus says the Lord, 'Did I indeed reveal myself to the house of your father when they were in Egypt subject to the house of Pharaoh?

28 Did I choose him out of all the tribes of Israel to be my priest, to go up to my altar, to burn incense, to wear an ephod before me? I gave to the house of your father all my offerings by fire from the people of Israel.

29 Why then do you scorn[b] my sacrifices and my offerings that I commanded for my dwelling, and honor your sons above me by fattening yourselves on the choicest parts of every offering of my people Israel?'

30 Therefore the Lord, the God of Israel, declares: 'I promised that your house and the house of your father should go in and out before me forever,' but now the Lord declares: 'Far be it from me, for those who honor me I will honor, and those who despise me shall be lightly esteemed.

31 Behold, the days are coming when I will cut off your strength and the strength of your father's house, so that there will not be an old man in your house.

32 Then in distress you will look with envious eye on all the prosperity that shall be bestowed on Israel, and there shall not be an old man in your house forever.

33 The only one of you whom I shall not cut off from my altar shall be spared to weep his[c] eyes out to grieve his heart, and all the descendants[d] of your house shall die by the sword of men.[e]

34 And this that shall come upon your two sons, Hophni and Phinehas, shall be the sign to you: both of them shall die on the same day.

35 And I will raise up for myself a faithful priest, who shall do according to what is in my heart and in my mind. And I will build him a sure house, and he shall go in and out before my anointed forever.

36 And everyone who is left in your house shall come to implore him for a piece of silver or a loaf of bread and shall say, "Please put me in one of the priests' places, that I may eat a morsel of bread."

This situation looks a whole lot like King Saul's and King David's, doesn't it? When I hear how some families are torn apart by death, drugs, alcohol, homosexuality, transgenderism, and other perversions, it breaks my heart to see they don't know their bloodline is being cut off! If the Father doesn't intervene, their lives are over, and so is the calling He had for their family. When the Father disregards a people, how great is the sorrow?

It may be ironic to think about how Samuel flourished during the time Eli was being judged. Eli was entrusted to train Samuel but was not able to teach his own sons. Have you ever had a coach or teacher who seemed to fail others but was able to help you? We cannot be so quick to throw people away because their children may have missed the mark or others that they have taught failed. God can still use them to show you something in your life if you allow Him. Eli was not perfect, neither was Samuel, and I am sure you nor I, but we all can be used and trusted to serve the Lord God.

Do you feel that you missed the mark? Have you been to more funerals than you count? Have you witnessed the sons that belong to your neighbors or perhaps your own and see how you may have failed them by not giving them Yah? When we should have been strong and steadfast, we were lenient and manipulated into being a friend instead of a parent to their detriment.

The hardest thing ever is to bury your child or children. I cannot imagine the pain, but there is a comforter that can help you process, accept, live, and learn from the lives and deaths of the people you love. The deaths of our children are not always our fault, of course, and it is not meant for us to blame ourselves. Eli was not to blame for his sons choosing to do the things they wanted to do. He was blamed for the lack of correction.

He suffered from not being the example of God's authority on earth. Some of the tears we cry at funerals are from our own failures, and if not, they should be. But don't cry and choose to do nothing. Get involved and help someone's child if you can no longer help your own. Wouldn't you have liked having someone there with you when you were trying to raise your children or dealing with them spinning out of control?

We don't get our experiences just to say we struggled here and there. We live and learn so that we can be of help and give a testimony to someone else. I am sure Eli had never cried like he did when God killed them both on the same day, but he also cried from the guilt he felt, the regret he felt, from making ***the biggest mistake that cost him everything***; but I am also sure he warned others not to do the same starting with Samuel.

C4

THE PRODIGAL'S SECOND CHANCE

The Prodigal Son was a parable in the New Testament that explains the love of a responsible father for his rebellious son. This son also grew tired of honoring his father, but unlike Eli, he was not allowed to live any kind of way at his house. He had to leave his house to live like a hellion, and that was what he chose to do.

<u>Luke 15:11-20 ESV</u>

11 And he said, "There was a man who had two sons.

12 And the younger of them said to his father, 'Father, give me the share of property that is coming to me.' And he divided his property between them.

13 Not many days later, the younger son gathered all he had and took a journey into a far country, and there he squandered his property in reckless living.

14 And when he had spent everything, a severe famine arose in that country, and he began to be in need.

15 So he went and hired himself out to[a] one of the citizens of that country, who sent him into his fields to feed pigs.

16 And he was longing to be fed with the pods that the pigs ate, and no one gave him anything.

17 "But when he came to himself, he said, 'How many of my father's hired servants have more than enough bread, but I perish here with hunger!

18 I will arise and go to my father, and I will say to him, "Father, I have sinned against heaven and before you.

19 I am no longer worthy to be called your son. Treat me as one of your hired servants.'"

20 And he arose and came to his father. But while he was still a long way off, his father saw him and felt compassion, and ran and embraced him and kissed him.

There was a standard set in the house of the prodigal son. He knew his dad was not going to give him anything until it was the appropriate time. I am also thinking that he thought he would not give him anything until he could be responsible for what he was to inherit. Sometimes, we think we are ready to get what our parents store up for us, don't we? We say what is taking them so long to give me what is mine? They need to get out of the way so that I can live and make my own decisions.

Have you seen how many new adults rush out of their parent's house only to need to come right back? These teenagers can't wait to turn eighteen so they can live how they think they want to and get somewhere they think they should be. This prodigal son had to learn the same lesson many young adults today are learning when they think of blowing their wealth on foolishness. When we desire to grow up fast, we can run the risk of not learning our purpose or missing it completely.

The prodigal son took the money his father worked for and disappeared from his home in a conceded manner. He told his father to die so he could get what was owed. It's funny how something currently in someone else's hand he felt entitled to. I have heard of too many cases where a parent spends all their money before they die and give their children nothing. Some give their money to their pets instead of their children or donate it to charity.

His father had a right to change his mind and give him nothing at any time; plus, he was the youngest son, so he could have given him nothing. He demanded something he didn't work for but was set up for him out of love. His father thought of making provisions for him, and the last thing on his son's mind was to give back to his father.

Have you seen ungrateful children make the biggest mistake to turn their backs on their parents? This son appeared to have a solid father, and not all children who rebel had a rough upbringing to justify how they think they should treat their parents. The Bible never said to be good to your parents if they are good to you, but it says to honor them with no asterisk (*Exodus 20:12*).

Are you honoring your parents with how you live and treat them? Do you visit them or call them to show you love and care for them? If they didn't leave you a dime, do you feel you don't have to care for them in their latter days? If they were never around for you, do you feel you can dismiss them like how they dismissed you? Would that be the will of God for you?

Before we treat people in any kind of way, we should know if this is what God would have for us to do. Would he want me to withhold what I could give to help? Would He be proud that I never call, post, write, visit, or text them? Is it enough for me to celebrate them only on Father's or Mother's Day?

Yes, parents can drive their children crazy, and boundaries may need to be in place to ensure peace, but we are to give honor where it is due. If it were not for them, we would not be here. Yah frequently calls Himself the God of your fathers, Abraham, Isaac, and Jacob, throughout the Bible. What is the importance of listing generations removed from the people He is talking to? I think it demonstrates how much time has passed and reminds His people to care about their history because that proves legacy matters.

This son left home and did everything he wanted to do. He went off and did everything he was big and bad to do. He drank his money away, spent it on women, and pleasured himself. He found himself broke after a while with no friends, no woman, and not one person cared about him after he couldn't make it rain anymore. He was no longer the big man, but a broke, penniless man! He had no home and was living amongst pigs, trying to scrape by.

He became homeless, jobless, penniless, and starving after he blew through his money. He squandered his wealth, but he remembered and came to himself. What a blessing it is to self-reflect and be honest about where you are. It is not so that you feel condemnation, but it is so you can see a way out. He was redeemed from a reprobated mindset so he could see his condition and mistakes.

The biggest mistake the prodigal son would have made if he kept going in this manner, was allowing pride to step between him and his purpose. He had a purpose at home. He had a loving home. Sometimes, you need to go home and rebuild. Sometimes, you need to learn more before you head out on your own, and that is okay. Sometimes, you take an entry position to understand how to become the manager somewhere else. You learn first to serve to appreciate those who will someday serve you.

Sometimes, we have to go work for someone else to better learn how to start and run our own businesses. He went back in humility, knowing he had failed God in heaven and his father. God really cares about how you treat your parents and those he puts over you. Everyone is not trying to hold you down but build you up. Allow the process to complete, and you will be ready for your purpose and the next steps to get there.

When he went home, he was welcomed with open arms. I know sometimes we go back to homes that don't welcome us with open arms. It might be with grunts, judgment, and lectures. Be patient and bear through the things that make you feel uncomfortable if they are intended to build your character.

Don't run from your life lessons, but embrace them and be all the wiser from them. Bless the people who blessed you, but have mercy on the people who also need mercy as you do. Maybe you are there to be the light for someone. Maybe you left your assignment too soon, so you had to return. Whatever you do for Yah, He will surely repay.

Unfortunately, not every son is like the prodigal and comes to their senses. Everyone who goes out in search of sin doesn't get the chance to realize their mistakes. There is a valuable lesson in kicking your children out of your house if they don't mind your rules. He had to go out and do his dirty work.

I know it is controversial for some to let their children leave when they know they are not ready to survive on their own. Sometimes, we do the right things, and still, bad things seem to happen. At times, a mother has to put her son or daughter out because they refuse to mind her rules.

This can save a life and sometimes bring more sadness. What the Father expects is for a line to be drawn for what the standard is. We are to train our children to follow that standard, but we cannot control them once they are adults. We have to allow them to make their choices and respect their decisions.

We don't have to permit things to happen in our homes that disrespect God's standards, so if we need to make that hard decision, we can trust leaning on God to do it. No parent wants to see their child fail. We may all take different approaches to achieve success, but trying means more than doing nothing to stop wicked behavior.

Not all children get the chance to return home and get right with their parents and God. Some die in the streets or in lifestyles they choose to have comfort in. We can still love our children and be a part of their lives even though we don't agree with their choices. We don't have to abandon people, but that may not stop them from leaving us as parents.

We are to pray over our children and entrust them to make the best decisions for their lives and souls. There is a chance that our children will die in the sins they loved more than God, but a greater calling is for them to wake up like the prodigal son to the holiness of Yah. Eli knew of the pain of losing his sons but also the holiness of Yah.

Yes, even though you may seem to be in disarray, children acting crazy, they are out in the streets, or if your life seems to be falling apart around you, you can still be used. Eli did great work in Samuel, much more than what he gave to his own sons. We should not be so quick to judge a person based on the outcomes of their children.

Likewise, we should not be so quick to assume that the outcome one person gets will be the same for another. Maybe Eli gave his sons the same training, but they just didn't want to listen to him. A student in one coach's hands can amount to more than in another. Is it the talent, the teacher, or the purpose that changes the outcomes?

Committing to developing your gifts is vital to you being in the will of God. Following God, we must decrease so that He can increase within us (*John 3:30*). Samuel and Saul were stewards for the Owner; the Owner is the Lord God Almighty because the earth belongs to Him, as do His people. We are all required to function in the body as His Spirit works overall and works through all and in all (*Ephesians 4:6*).

DELIVERER

C5

MOSES, PHAROAH, AND YAH'S WRATH

What Hannah prayed in *1 Samuel* chapter *2* and verse *10* set the tone for the case of Moses. Moses was born at a time when the people needed Yah in a serious way. The enslaved Hebrews were forced to work without remorse to the point of exhaustion, to make them feel inferior and doubt their place with God. In Hannah's prayer, she said,

> "The adversaries of the Lord shall be broken to pieces;
>
> against them, He will thunder in heaven.
>
> The Lord will judge the ends of the earth;
>
> He will give strength to His king
>
> and exalt the horn of His anointed."

How profound were her words? Her words give the very structure and performance of God's amazing deliverance of His people from the grip of Pharoah in the land of Egypt. Many think they can trouble you and keep you a slave for as long as they want to, but Yah says, "Not so!" Even though God is a good God who judges His children, do not be fooled into believing that in your season of judgment, His love has departed from you.

A good father corrects his children when they have errored. How much more so should the Father of all nationalities, peoples, universes, and galaxies? His ways are higher surely as the heavens are higher than earth (*Isaiah 55:9*).

He promised His people they would be enslaved in Egypt because they went after other gods. These gods were any and everything that took them off the track from seeking His will for their lives. You see when the shepherds got to Egypt, they were at first still doing what they were accustomed to doing. But do you know how they ended up working in a pyramid?

Do you think God called them to go and become builders? Some of you were born to be shepherds, warriors, farmers, priests (pastors), prophets, psalmists, doctors, lawyers, craftsmen, housewives, mothers, fathers, sisters, and brothers. These talents were given to you to lift up the saints and impact the world for Yah. Tell me, what happens to a people who lose their skilled workers because they want to become like everyone around them?

What happens when the people who were content with what they had now desire what someone else had? What happens when the brands you have you now feel don't measure up to other brands? Your leagues don't seem as impactful as their leagues. What happens when your customers are not as desirable as having their customers? What happens when you seek someone else's approval instead of God's approval?

You end up crossing over to take a job in the temple when you should be working in the field. You end up leaving your people, communities, and leagues in search of other opportunities. You end up working in a pyramid to obtain shinner things that are gold but lose your soul, culture, and position. You obtain riches and wealth for a season, but you are tormented now in your sleep.

You were a free soul, but now, your children are bought and paid for by the enemy. You cannot go as you please for fear of the paparazzi. You cannot buy what you want because they give you a list of stores you must support. You cannot speak your thoughts or you will be canceled and made to look like you went insane. They lift your name in lights and burn them on television screens when you step out of line.

The same way these people were pressed down and looked to be delivered is where communities are today. We should be lifting our eyes up to heaven because we realize how far away from God we have moved. They went from making money to being forced to work for free. It appeared that the Egyptians were working just as hard as them until, slowly but surely, they pulled themselves from the pyramid and left the Hebrews behind.

This reminds me of the women's suffrage movement and how white and black women began to work together to fight for women's rights. In the beginning, they both were complaining together. They both were voicing their views about men and their ability to be independent together. Then something happened: the black women were still talking about being superwomen, but the white woman did not appear to leave her home.

The white woman found a balance to maintain the home with her freedoms better than black women who shot a gun through her own roof to be heard. She cut down her man to the point where he no longer wanted to be around and couldn't be if she received government support. She burned the institution of marriage in exchange for government support and child support. She became a single parent by choice. She permitted the idea of abortion to be shared with her daughters, introduced by the racist Margret Sanger, under the guise of freedom and control.

The Levites were not duped into working inside the pyramid-like their brethren. They remained in their position and never worked inside the pyramids. Yah showed them more mercy than those who left their post in search of things, riches, and customs of the Egyptians. Not all the tribes built the pyramids; however, all the tribes suffered as a unit and were pushed to ghettos when their land was taken by the Pharoah.

What would a man do who fears being a has-been more than God? He would issue a decree to enslave a people so that they would not turn against them in battle and escape out of the land.

Exodus 1:9-14 KJV

9 And he said unto his people, Behold, the people of the children of Israel are more and mightier than we:

10 Come on, let us deal wisely with them; lest they multiply, and it come to pass, that, when there falleth out any war, they join also unto our enemies, and fight against us, and so get them up out of the land.

11 Therefore they did set over them taskmasters to afflict them with their burdens. And they built for Pharaoh treasure cities, Pithom and Raamses.

12 But the more they afflicted them, the more they multiplied and grew. And they were grieved because of the children of Israel.

13 And the Egyptians made the children of Israel to serve with rigour:

14 And they made their lives bitter with hard bondage, in morter, and in brick, and in all manner of service in the field: all their service, wherein they made them serve, was with rigour.

The Pharoah did an assessment to compare his people to that of the Hebrews. When he did the assessment, he found facts that made him feel inferior to this race of people. Instead of dealing wisely with them to make offers to keep them, he decided to deal wickedly instead.

He did not want to lose what authority he had

over his land, and his biggest mistake was that he assumed that everything on his land belonged to him. When you work a job, exist in a marriage, compete in a competition, or represent a brand, company, and similar, it's funny how these entities presume they can tell you how to live. It is as if you are their possession, and the works you create belong to them also.

I know some companies claim any ideas you come up with on the clock at their premises they own, too! How wicked to assume someone else's ideas and creativity you can swoop in and take because they work for you. Or if they live on your land, etc. But how many inventors were harmed during slavery and into today with people taking their ideas because they were unaware of how to protect them? This terrible thinking made Pharoah make the biggest mistake for his people, which, in time, cost them everything!

Some things don't sprout up when you plant them. Some plants and trees take years to root in the ground before coming up. When they shoot forth, wow, the sight is amazing, and the fruit is too. A bamboo tree takes 3 years to root and can grow several feet in a day when it sprouts from the ground.

Likewise, an apple tree also takes years to root, but the fruit you grow is so much better than the fruit you buy, most gardeners say. I remember my neighbors having apple trees, and I loved picking the fresh apples and seeing where my food came from. No wax, pesticides, or questionable harvesting when you do it yourself.

The question we all must ask ourselves is, what are the roots being planted in our lives? In the case of Eli, his sons planted deep roots of hideous fruit. Their works were unfruitful and would only grow sour fruit–even deadly. Just because the judgment is not instantaneous doesn't mean the action is of no effect. How long do some of us wait to turn our lives around and expect a miracle or mercy?

We will spend 60 years smoking and expect Yah to do a miraculous healing on our lungs because we refused to discipline ourselves. Is it wrong if the Father says, this is what you planted? Does He not love you if He allows you to suffer from your own fault? Is He supposed to only function to help you dodge bullets you knew had your name on them?

Or is He allowed to be sovereign in your life? Is he allowed to correct and punish if He says it is necessary? Do you allow Him to give and take away? The Father gave His people Moses as an answer to their prayers because He had a plan for His life.

None of us are here just because, but we are all an answer to each other's prayers. The people prayed for deliverance, and the Father sent them a deliverer who, too, needed deliverance. Amazing how imperfect people can be used to accomplish such great things, is it not?

When the pressure-packed on, the people multiplied all the more. The bug that many thought they could eliminate to keep control quickly realized this great nation has something on its side beyond man. Normally, if you separate a people, they will die off or dwindle in numbers at least. Yet, when God blesses a people, even during times of harsh punishment, rebuke, slavery, and correction, they multiply.

It was normal for Pharoah to fear a people he could not control. An even greater fear was to wonder, what could these people do somewhere else if they were not here under his feet? Not only could they war with him, but he feared being under their feet someday. Nobody likes it when the tables turn. They wonder if you will be as harsh as they were. Will you show mercy? This worriment is enough to torment.

So Moses comes, and he survives an edict to kill all male Hebrew children. The midwives and his mother hid him from Pharoah to allow him to grow. When he was too old to hide, she gave her the basket holding her son to Myriam to sit on the river. On this river, the daughter of the Pharoah drew the baby boy out of the water and thought to keep him.

She asked the Pharoah, and he agreed to her keeping Moses. She sent this beloved child to the woman who birthed him to feed and provide for him (*Exodus 2:9*). It brought his mother great joy to provide for her son in plain sight with no fear of punishment.

> **9** And Pharaoh's daughter said unto her, Take this child away, and nurse it for me, and I will give thee thy wages. And the women took the

child and nursed it.

What is amazing, she paid his mother to do something she would have done for free. The princess knew that she was the mother of Moses and didn't penalize her for going against the Pharoah's edict. If this doesn't prove there is a God, what would? When you are faithful, the things you would do for free the Father will bless you for doing! What you do out of obedience, Yah will make a way for you because you were faithful to your assignment.

Everyone in the Bible has flaws, committed sins, and fallen short of the glory of Yah, but there are some people in the Bible and in the world that the Father loves because He does. They can get one thing or many things right and do plenty of things wrong, and He will still bless them.

King David was not a stellar man. He made fatal mistakes. He killed a man, stole someone's wife, had plenty of side-chicks, did a census on Yah's people, and people died because of his mistakes. Yet! God used him for a great work. He blessed him even though his children were not stellar examples of Kingdom Living. He did something right to be a man after God's Heart, and even though he messed up, some would argue daily (*1 Samuel 13:14*).

King David was not perfect, and neither was Moses. Moses was a man raised with benefits other Hebrews didn't have. He was raised to be friends with the Pharoah's children. Although he knew he had a different position, he never forgot he was a Hebrew. He never acted as if he was greater than his fellow man. He never turned his back on them, but he did have to learn how to politic with the enemy, who was also his friend and adopted grandfather.

In the book of Jasher it shows an account of Moses that I do think is worth sharing to help understand Moses a bit better. If you don't read this book or disregard the contents, it won't change the outcome of this chapter or take away from the life of Moses. If you were to read the book and take into account what was written, you would find this.

When Moses was a baby being brought to the palace to live with his adopted Egyptian mother, a magician saw a sight that troubled him. While the Pharaoh was holding the baby, the baby took the crown off of his head. Not intending to overstep his boundary, the magician gasped in astonishment at the sight along with others watching.

Jasher 70:1-9

> **1** And in the third year from the birth of Moses, Pharaoh was sitting at a banquet, when Alparanith the queen was sitting at his right and Bathia at his left, and the lad Moses was lying upon her bosom, and Balaam the son of Beor with his two sons, and all the princes of the kingdom were sitting at table in the king's presence.

> **2** And the lad stretched forth his hand upon the king's head, and took the crown from the king's head and placed it on his own head.

> **3** And when the king and princes saw the work

which the boy had done, the king and princes were terrified, and one man to his neighbor expressed astonishment.

4 And the king said unto the princes who were before him at table, What speak you and what say you, O ye princes, in this matter, and what is to be the judgment against the boy on account of this act?

5 And Balaam the son of Beor the magician answered before the king and princes, and he said, Remember now, O my lord and king, the dream which thou didst dream many days since, and that which thy servant interpreted unto thee.

6 Now therefore this is a child from the Hebrew children, in whom is the spirit of God, and let not my lord the king imagine that this youngster did this thing without knowledge.

7 For he is a Hebrew boy, and wisdom and understanding are with him, although he is yet a child, and with wisdom has he done this and chosen unto himself the kingdom of Egypt.

8 For this is the manner of all the Hebrews to deceive kings and their nobles, to do all these things cunningly, in order to make the kings of the earth and their men tremble.

9 Surely thou knowest that Abraham their father acted thus, who deceived the army of Nimrod king of Babel, and Abimelech king of Gerar, and that he possessed himself of the land of the children of Heth and all the kingdoms of Canaan.

The first eye-catching moment has to be why a Hebrew child is sitting in the lap of an Egyptian King. Next, why is a Hebrew manchild sitting in the lap of an Egyptian king? The Pharoah playing with the boy is, in fact, a slap in his own face as he passed the law to have all Hebrew boys killed at birth, and here he plays with one that was not. He also supported raising the child and bringing him close to his own bosom. There is only One who can make you look like a fool and make you unaware at this level.

The king was content with playing with this handsome child. He never thought this baby would have anything to do with his dreams, fears, or the plan that Yah had already devised to deliver His people. He only saw a cute baby. Some things in our lives that we allow to sit in our laps may appear to be cute in their infancy, but when fully grown, they will turn on us. In this case, the turning was in Yah's favor, but what if the turning was against you?

We say God is cruel when He tells His warriors to kill off people. We said it didn't sit right with us, like King Saul said, for God to kill everybody. We wanted to find some humane thing about saving a life or preserving a people. Only Yah knows that the one you saved alive would come back and kill you or bring more trouble to your doorstep. So He said to cut it off, but how often do we save things alive?

Do we stay in relationships that should go? Do we hold on to jobs that we know are behind us? Or clinging to concepts of thought, holding rocks, stones, and ideas from the world He pulled us out of? Rachel couldn't let the wood pieces (gods) her father cherished go. It cost her life to hide them away from her father, and it was by accident her own husband had to kill her. Sometimes, the people you love are the same ones you have to cut off.

Yet, in the mercy of Yah, he gave Rachel children for Israel's (Jacob's) sake, His purpose, and our benefit. Without Joseph, the Hebrews wouldn't have been in Egypt to begin with, and the people would not have been spared from widespread famine. It may look weird, even bad, but God can show mercy where He chooses. He can deliver you by bringing you home or killing you and putting you in hell.

He can use anything and anyone to achieve His divine purpose and will. This magician did not know Yah, and he was a worker of the enemy whom God allowed to understand the dream Pharoah had. Joseph said the interpretation of dreams belongs to the Father (*Genesis 40:8*). The Father can use anyone to give a word, and those that are His and those that are not are all vessels used for His purpose (*2 Timothy 2:20-23*).

Moses, as a child, had what he needed within him to please Yah. He had the Almighty on his side–even living within Him as a baby when he didn't know how to mature his gift. Raw talent, raw destiny, lit up the room for those who could perceive it. Not everyone who sees your light comes in peace. Some see how bright you shine and want to snuff out the light and the hope of the people praying for you.

People are not praying for the perfect you. They are praying for someone who can understand them. People who know what it is like to suffer are in need, want, and need help. Christ came to earth, so He also understands betrayal, suffering, disappointment, and pain. He can relate to every disease, hurt, and atrocity because He bore them all on the cross.

Moses was not perfect in the sight of men, but he was perfect in the sight of Yah.

Jasher 70:18-30

18 Now therefore my lord king behold this child has risen up in their stead in Egypt, to do according to their deeds and to trifle with every king, prince and judge.

19 If it please the king, let us now spill his blood upon the ground, lest he grow up and take away the government from thy hand, and the hope of Egypt perish after he shall have reigned.

20 And Balaam said to the king, Let us moreover call for all the judges of Egypt and the wise men thereof, and let us know if the judgment of death is due to this boy as thou didst say, and then we will slay him.

21 And Pharaoh sent and called for all the wise men of Egypt and they came before the king, and an angel of the Lord came amongst them, and he was like one of the wise men of Egypt.

22 And the king said to the wise men, Surely you have heard what this Hebrew boy who is in the house has done, and thus has Balaam judged in the matter.

23 Now judge you also and see what is due to the boy for the act he has committed.

24 And the angel, who seemed like one of the wise men of Pharaoh, answered and said as follows, before all the wise men of Egypt and before the king and the princes:

25 If it please the king let the king send for men who shall bring before him an onyx stone and a coal of fire, and place them before the child, and if the child shall stretch forth his hand and take the onyx stone, then shall we know that with wisdom has the youth done all that he has done, and we must slay him.

26 But if he stretch forth his hand upon the coal, then shall we know that it was not with knowledge that he did this thing, and he shall live.

27 And the thing seemed good in the eyes of the king and the princes, so the king did according to the word of the angel of the Lord.

28 And the king ordered the onyx stone and coal to be brought and placed before Moses.

29 And they placed the boy before them, and the lad endeavored to stretch forth his hand to the onyx stone, but the angel of the Lord took his hand and placed it upon the coal, and the coal became extinguished in his hand, and he lifted it up and put it into his mouth, and burned part of his lips and part of his tongue, and he became heavy in mouth and tongue.

30 And when the king and princes saw this, they knew that Moses had not acted with wisdom in taking off the crown from the king's head.

Moses and many of us think we have imperfections because we committed a sin or deserve what happened to us. What if the suffering, the thorn in our side, was to keep us hidden in plain sight? Do you think a perfect Moses would have lived long in the sight of Pharoah? Do you think a glorious man with perfect speech, stature, intellect, and godly behavior would be able to live in peace among Egyptians?

Consider the life of Joseph again. A married woman lusted after his beauty to the point she would rather see him dead than not entertain her nasty thoughts towards him. A man who appeared to be of natural perfection would have troubled the Pharoah, and he would have killed him if he had seen him as a threat. His speech made him fly under the radar, as my mom would say.

Don't hate your humble beginnings. Don't hate your short hair, your simple features, your simple language, your simple neighborhood, your simple education, or anything you feel makes you less than perfect. Your being less than perfect makes you a perfect tool for God to invade territories that are not as accessible to warriors!

Never think you are nothing because you

don't have a perfect background. You come with scars, stretchmarks, and imperfections. You are fearfully and wonderfully made! You are called for a time such as this. There were no mistakes as to why you are here, and your assignment doesn't change because you feel you are not worthy.

Moses was enough for God, but he was quickly kicked out of Pharoah's camp when he made a wrong turn. Have you ever been the go-to person, and you made one wrong turn and found yourself ousted? Some people have business models that don't mind preying on Hebrew people, but the moment you prey on them, they turn their back and let you fall.

It's okay for you to rap music that talks about killing your own people, saying your women are female dogs. Seeing your sons dress like women and your daughters like prostitutes. The theys of the world don't mind you sitting in their laps and playing with their crowns if they believe you are no threat. You are nothing more than a tamed baby tiger in their eyes. But do know, their eyes are on you, and they will always be suspicious of you until you are put out of sight.

I believe the Pharoah also intended to use Moses to his benefit. The slavery of the days of Moses, I believe, has some similarities to that of the enslavement of Hebrews in America. Just like Harriet Tubman was described as black Moses, I think her people can be likened to the Hebrews of old. Slave masters did not mind taking a few blacks to lift up to make the other blacks envy those blacks, and what happens is jealousy, strife, and division.

A united people, families in arms, tribes in arms, and people (like in the tower of Bable) in arms are hard to defeat. Yah, the Almighty One even says who could oppose them if they were to all link together (*Genesis 11:6*)? Of course, the Almighty God can oppose them and He struck the tower and confused languages to ensure people could not gather in such a way again orchestrated by man, but it is permitted in Him by His Spirit.

15 Now when Pharaoh heard this thing, he sought to slay Moses. But Moses fled from the face of Pharaoh and dwelt in the land of Midian: and he sat down by a well.

If Moses had killed a Hebrew man, nothing likely would have happened to him (*Exodus 2:15*). But to have killed an Egyptian man, it was wise for him to fear for his life and leave. I am sure if the Pharoah's son or anyone from the palace killed an Egyptian soldier under similar circumstances, he would not have been put to death. It is in these times we realize, if we were asleep, that the eyes of the enemy never left their pet tiger.

The Pharoah didn't seek to reason with Moses to understand why he killed an Egyptian. Law and order, or the patience to find out this matter and show the same regard he would for his son, was not part of the equation. He treated Moses like an enemy at that moment and not a son. Even if Moses was in the wrong, something weird would have been celebrated, like how strong he was, brave, and warriorlike, if he were, in fact, regarded by the king as a son.

When you are seen as an adorned slave, your strengths intimidate those who sought to keep you under their feet. They cannot have their poster child for the Hebrew race usurp authority over the current ruling party. Moses was not only speaking for himself but was an example for the entire Hebrew race. When he rose up and slew an Egyptian, the Pharoah surely thought the Hebrew people would rise up and do the same.

Why do you think all the strong leaders are killed, but not only in the US all over the world? Why are people coerced to change their views to the leading rule? Why do you think people who have a word for their people are soon snuffed out and killed by their own governments? Why do you think advocates of freedom, change, and equality are feared more than people of war, death, and murder? Did you know Martin Luther King Jr.'s mother was shot in church and assassinated in broad daylight?

Gangs can walk freely in the streets, but a nonviolent march will bring out the Armed Guard! Clubs can operate message parlors known for prostitutes and money laundering without a peep from too many police. Women can cross oceans in steel containers without being picked up on radar for weeks and years on end. Drugs are brought over on planes and snuck through borders; sex traffickers and organ harvesters seem to have passports to reach any land with no checks.

Hardly a thing is spoken or done. The people of The world don't mind evil going forth because they see that as justification for their existence, one can believe. The sex trafficking industry, modern-day slavery, accounts for 150 billion dollars each year. The United States spends 90 million to combat it annually. Imagine countries that don't spend a dime and now consider if they all did. Now we can better understand why organized crime exists and is more prevalent than justice.

Crime they see as a means to justify law and order, bills, police, and politicians. But when you are able to manage yourselves, they dismantle your parties. They call your leaders terrorists. When you defy the almighty armies from pillaging your villages and separating your families, they call you a dictator and a hater of men.

If you regulate what is right or wrong for your children, they call you an unfit parent while they tell them a girl can be a boy and a boy a girl. They tell you that homosexuality is natural and pedophiles should have rights. They blur the lines of public bathrooms and don't arrest prostitutes on the streets (many of which are underage and likely trafficked). When you come together to better your communities, when you join in arms to stand for positive change, they call that a riot!

Do you understand now why people are reluctant to train you? Why games are played and you don't know the players' names, the rules, or how to win or lose? But you are the game you play while being lulled to sleep, believing there is peace in the world as long as my children are okay. But people are reluctant to train you because they see a pattern in the Father's ways.

He will have you raise up your replacement. If you understand Yah, you will celebrate the opportunity, but if you are in judgment, you will be bitter like King Saul and the Pharoah. Not everybody likes a change of a season when the change means their kingdom comes to an end.

It was not only the Egyptians who feared judgment; it was the Romans, the Greeks, the Philistines, the Assyrians, the Babylonians, and many more who had kingdoms they never thought would end or slow down. People who have been playing a long game of monopoly with God the almighty, taking lands, and people as real estate, erecting their buildings and cities to push His children into ghettos. The Pharoah took prime real estate from the Hebrews when he pushed them out. He put them in ghettos and thought because they saw poverty all around them, they would believe they were worthless like their living conditions.

He thought by changing what you see that would change what you believe! He thought by taking away the voice of your God on public displays and giving you no time to gather among yourselves or in temples, your purpose and connection with Yah would fade away. He thought that you would come to know the gods of the Egyptians and worship the things they value, he in fact, rewired you for his purpose and will.

Even though we are folded under cultures that live contrary to the calling of Yah and have become a byword in all the nations as promised, it doesn't mean God has forsaken His promise. This is the evidence that He is God because everything He said would be has become. But what many omit from your history is the part where we rise! Where you are delivered, you are set free!

We may think about how God would have His people suffer in slavery for 400 years but don't realize there was still grace and mercy there. He could have started over like He wanted to do with Moses. He could have cast people aside, but instead, he chose to toil and wrestle with us as an angel did with Jacob (Israel).

When Moses fled with a plan to go who knows where he found favor with Ethiopians. He was married and lived a life of peace for many years. He had distanced himself from his past as much as he could, but his purpose wasn't to be born, spared, or raised by the king but to go and live among people in peace. He was raised up to be a tool, a battle ax in the hand of Yah to deliver His people.

Do you know sometimes, when you make it out of the hood, it isn't for you? It is not always meant for you to make it out and turn your back on the people you left behind. As I visited Gary, Indiana, I could only think, could you imagine what could have been done with this city if the talent raised from it would have given back? If they had built a center and provided a grant to help with aging houses instead of fencing off their property and leaving the community behind, where could Gary be?

This is the proposed King of Pop, and his hometown is a ghost town with nothing but a gated house in his memory. The entire downtown is holding on by a thread. When the mill shut down, so did the city in many ways. Making matters worse, he nor his family built anything there. However, Michael built a theme park on the other side of the world that these children will likely never see. Never, never land was accurate, for how many will never see his memory like it could have been until he reaches back into the soil. They will never, never see it.

Why, when people get comfortable, do they forget about the people who sacrificed for them? Moses's mom risked her life, and so did her family to raise him. His sister stuck her neck out to ensure he ended where he was supposed to be. But here is Moses living life and falling asleep in peace while his community suffers. The Jacksons lived their interesting life while their home city fell to pieces without a peep. So many rich black neighborhoods were brought to nothing through racism. Tulsa, Oklahoma, makes the list, and these two cases are not an anomaly.

The Father set a bush on fire to get Moses's attention! He came close to see what was going on with the bush, but I can imagine God had already tried to speak to Him, but he muted the still, quiet voice. Has Yah called your name using people, movies, friends, or family, and you ignored it? Does he have to do something outrageous to get your attention?

Exodus 3:2-4 ESV

> **2** And the angel of the Lord appeared to him in a flame of fire out of the midst of a bush. He looked, and behold, the bush was burning, yet it was not consumed.
>
> **3** And Moses said, "I will turn aside to see this great sight, why the bush is not burned."
>
> **4** When the Lord saw that he turned aside to see, God called to him out of the bush, "Moses, Moses!" And he said, "Here I am."

It is pretty hard to ignore Yah when you are witnessing a burning bush not being consumed. Hard to miss if you know you should have been dead but are alive, and equally hard to miss him when you see your life going one way, but He re-routed you another way. When the Father pursues you, it is hard to miss Him.

Sometimes, when He seeks to find us, we aren't thinking anything about what His plans are for our lives. Like Moses, we were just living and not thinking about home. Then, he was asked to go back, but he didn't know how to do that. I am sure fear gripped him. He asked questions like how do I prove that you are sending me? Who do I say has sent me? With what power do I have to go to your people or Egyptians to do anything? I am sure he thought I was a wanted man. How could I ever go back? But the instructions were the same.

Your fear or insecurities doesn't stop what your calling is. If the Father sets you apart to do a thing, that is what He has done. He told Moses everything he already knew: He was with him, wants to use him, and everything he knows will help Yah's children. Everything you learn, the Father can use to advance His Kingdom. If you learned how to take care of animals, feed your family, work a job, fix your credit, buy and sell property, government, nutrition, customer service, medical, and everything in between, He can use it!

Have you ever gotten called and all you can think of is they? They won't believe it. They won't like how I talk. They won't like how I dress. They won't accept me because of this or that, and to help with your little faith, God gives you more. They will say I am not studied enough to preach, so He sends you to school. We forget that you should first be called.

They will say I don't wear suits, but we forget neither did the Messiah! I am not a man or woman with great vocabulary and eloquent speech, but Moses stuttered and the simple things the Lord loves to use to confound the wise (*1 Corinthians 1:27*). When we decrease and it is not about what we are wearing, how long our hair is, where we are from, and how much we have, we can move out of the way so that Yah may get the glory.

Moses could perform signs and wonders, but he didn't do them for his own glory. He did every sign for the edification and fulfillment of Yah's glory. He was obedient to perform each action in the sight of Pharoah. He warned and warned again, but the Pharoah had a deaf ear to hear and blind eyes to perceive what Yah wanted.

The truth, like with Eli's sons, it pleased the Lord to harden the Pharoah's heart so that He could bring about judgment on the Egyptians. Many preach the merciful God that He is but forget that He is a righteous God that judges man and their hearts. The Pharoah denying the freedom of Yah's people was the biggest mistake he could ever make!

He not only said no once, twice, but several times over several days and lived through too many unnatural acts to think he could fight a God like this. Have you ever seen people who looked past the divine facts for what they wanted? They don't care who gets harmed and killed, or what they lose in the moment. They can only see what they perceive as a victory. This tunnel vision killed the firstborn in every family, in every field, and throughout the land of Egypt.

It wasn't until the death of people that the Israelites were freed. They allowed their streams to turn into blood, lost their livestock, and lived with lice and frogs. The locust ate up their vegetation. They saw drought, large balls of hail crush their roofs, and still didn't bow! Is that strength or pure arrogance? Not only did these people lose greatly, but they also pursued the Hebrews, thinking of bringing them back to help them again!

They thought the three days were over, so now, come back Hebrews and serve us (I am sure they wanted to say), but the sea swallowed them alive before they could demand it. The enemies of Yah's children have limitations on what they can do. Once the Father sets you free, you are free indeed (*John 8:36*). So cling to the promise of freedom. Cling to the promise of change. Repent by changing your mind so that you won't make the biggest mistake you can make, and that is to miss the shift of Yah for your future.

C6

AFTER THE RED
SEA

Have you ever wondered what happened to the Pharoah after the Red Sea? I mean, did they all die in the sea? Did God have no mercy on anybody? I mean, Yah stiffened the neck of Pharoah, so he was a vessel, but was there really no hope for this pharaoh?

Would it surprise you if there were hope for this broken king? A king who can now better relate to Moses than he ever thought he would. A king that now has a people that he knows hates his guts. I am sure they cannot stand him because he cost them everything.

They lost their homes, children, livestock, water, fields, and even their slaves and servants. They went from living on top to sinking fast! How could he ever show his face back at home if, in fact, he was to blame for every firstborn dying throughout the land? I am sure he felt lower than low. He would have also been the last to enter the water, allowing his guards to go before him.

So, if he hadn't entered the water or made it out alive, would he have had a similar life to Esau, Cain, or someone God hates? Would you be surprised to know Yah shows mercy on whom He chooses to have mercy (*Romans 9:15-16*)? We don't control who Yah chooses to save. Nineveh He chose to save, Paul he chose to save, Peter he chose to save, and the Pharoah, He chose to save.

Jasher 81:39-42

> **39** And the Lord manifested to the children of Israel his wonders in Egypt and in the sea by the hand of Moses and Aaron.
>
> **40** And when the children of Israel had entered the sea, the Egyptians came after them, and the waters of the sea resumed upon them, and they all sank in the water, and not one man was left excepting Pharaoh, who gave thanks to the Lord and believed in him, therefore the Lord did not cause him to perish at that time with the Egyptians.
>
> **41** And the Lord ordered an angel to take him from amongst the Egyptians, who cast him upon the land of Ninevah, and he reigned over it for a long time.
>
> **42** And on that day the Lord saved Israel from the hand of Egypt, and all the children of Israel saw that the Egyptians had perished, and they beheld the great hand of the Lord, in what he had performed in Egypt and in the sea.

Have you ever seen someone make it and thought to yourself, they should be dead? Why did the Father show mercy on that guy or that woman?

Why does the Father save murderers, robbers, adulterers, and people who do wrong? Why did Yah save King David? He was all of those things and some, but the Father chose to have mercy.

You can see a person dying in the movies, and somehow he comes back, and you say, "Man, he should have died! He deserved to die," but we do not know what we speak. On the cross, the Messiah said forgive them for they do not know what they do (*Luke 23:34*). We entertain angels unaware the Bible says (*Hebrews 13:2*). Has an angel pulled you out from sinking?

Has someone reached into your life when you were thought to be dead and brought you back? Were you out with a gang, doing everything they were doing, but you didn't go to jail? Have you been in a car accident, and everyone else in the car died, but you were saved alive? Have you seen families buried in rubble, and you make it, and others don't? Have you ever lost your whole family because you turned to believe the truth and others chose to believe a lie? Have you opted to follow Yah while others cursed you for not following yourself or satan?

It is hard sometimes to come to yourself and say, "Father, I need you. Forgive me, have mercy on me," when you know you don't deserve it. If anyone should have died in the sea, surely it should have been the king leading the way! You may have been the ring leader in an argument, instigated a fight, or caused the division, yet the Father sent you an angel.

Not only did He pull you out of the hood, the

ghetto, the gang, the burning building, the toppled business, off drugs (addictions), an unloving marriage, abusive connection, or poverty, but He sat you over something else. He trusted you to rule! He gave you a house to command. A healthy body to maintain. A loving family to build you up and a team of folks to support your vision.

Who wouldn't want to serve a God like this? I absolutely love the song "Nobody Like You Lord" by Maranda Curtis. I love the life account of Helen Baylor, which shows how the Father saved her life and her husband's. A great song she made about her testimony, "Praying Grandmother." The power of the Almighty is something that cannot be explained and truly surpasses our understanding.

When we think we get who He wants, He does something with someone like Noah. He took a drunk and redeemed humanity with him! What an awesome God! This same God can work wonders with you and me. I love the song by Tye Tribbett, "He Turned It." For some of us, the devil thinks he has you because you are roped up in evil, addiction, depression, poverty, and hatred, but God!

Let Him turn it for you!

LOVE

SAMSON'S
DEADLY LOVE
FOR THE
FORBIDDEN

Samson was one of the greatest gifts his mother received. His father and mother did not have children before him because she was barren. Like Hannah, his mother wanted children, but she was patient, and God sent an angel to her with the message.

Judges 13:2-7 ESV

2 There was a certain man of Zorah, of the tribe of the Danites, whose name was Manoah. And his wife was barren and had no children.

3 And the angel of the Lord appeared to the woman and said to her, "Behold, you are barren and have not borne children, but you shall conceive and bear a son.

4 Therefore be careful and drink no wine or strong drink, and eat nothing unclean,

5 for behold, you shall conceive and bear a son. No razor shall come upon his head, for the child shall be a Nazirite to God from the womb, and he shall begin to save Israel from the hand of the Philistines."

6 Then the woman came and told her husband,

"A man of God came to me, and his appearance was like the appearance of the angel of God, very awesome. I did not ask him where he was from, and he did not tell me his name,

7 but he said to me, 'Behold, you shall conceive and bear a son. So then drink no wine or strong drink, and eat nothing unclean, for the child shall be a Nazirite to God from the womb to the day of his death.'"

She was faithful to listen and to obey, as was Manoah, her husband, a Danite. They knew that, like Moses's mother, they had an exceptional child who was born for a purpose. Do you know the children you are privileged to have are also born with purpose? Before we were formed in our mother's womb, the Almighty knew us and called us to a purpose (*Jeremiah 1:5*).

This angel confirmed what we all should know: no one is here by accident, and all that we do can be turned to the glory of Yah. Isn't it amazing that of all the women for Samson to decide he wanted, he picked a Philistine woman?

His parents tried to sway him because they knew this would likely bring trouble. Yet, we read this trouble was what Yah wanted.

Judges 14:1-4 ESV

1 Samson went down to Timnah, and at Timnah, he saw one of the daughters of the Philistines.

2 Then he came up and told his father and mother, "I saw one of the daughters of the Philistines at Timnah. Now get her for me as my wife."

3 But his father and mother said to him, "Is there not a woman among the daughters of your relatives, or among all our people, that you must go to take a wife from the uncircumcised Philistines?" But Samson said to his father, "Get her for me, for she is right in my eyes."

4 His father and mother did not know that it was from the Lord, for he was seeking an opportunity against the Philistines. At that time, the Philistines ruled over Israel.

This love was a forbidden one, like in Romeo and Juliet, a black man wanting a white woman in the 1920s and earlier. This love, lust, or interest his parents knew would cause trouble of some kind. Yet, and still, his parents did not deny him. His father took him to the land for which Samson saw a potential bride.

Have your parents ever told you, "No son (daughter), I don't think this would be a good fit for you?" Did you listen, or were you like Samson, and did you believe your own desires should come first? Were you oblivious to how your choices could impact others and the troubles the relationship could bring?

Samson was motivated to come against the Philistines; rightfully, it was part of his purpose, but the timing was everything, right? Have you ever noticed the right woman or man can come into your life and encourage you to go places you wouldn't have gone had you not met them? There is a song by one of the Jonas brothers saying how a woman is tearing up his reputation.

Have you ever chased someone who is or would tear up your reputation? We live in a world where reputation and a good name, as the Bible calls it, are prized possessions. Even the disciples didn't want to be caught with people that would compromise their reputation. Remember how Peter tried to separate himself from new converts when people challenged his reputation?

The Pharisees tried to convince him to put the same burdens the Hebrews had on the Gentiles. Paul had to rebuke Peter about this because the Father saves both the Hebrew and the Greek. He never mandated that the Gentiles have to do the same things as the Hebrews.

Not all of us will have the same responsibilities, and what some of us can do, others cannot. We may think hair is no big deal, drinking, or if you choose to smoke, etc. Yashua turned water into wine. Why would He do that if the wine was so terrible? Why would the Bible have scriptures that say to drink and make your heart merry if, in fact, no one can or should (*Ecclesiastes 9:7-8*)?

The truth, everyone doesn't have to refrain from wine. If that were the case, Yashua, at the wedding, should have condemned all of their actions, including His own! There is not one scripture that implies He did such a thing. Yet we condemn people for drinking more than being sober-minded, holy, or drunk.

Samson could not drink at all because he was a Nazarene. Nazarites cannot drink wine or vinegar or eat grapes from the vine. They are to be a holy people set apart for Yah's great work. *Numbers 6:1-21* further outline the requirements to include not touching any deadly thing, cutting your hair, drinking alcohol, and to be holy (likely meaning celibacy).

Holiness was often associated with being celibate if living as a Nazarite. Like how Yashua was a Nazarene who was holy and set apart, and some argue that Paul was as well. Perhaps this is why Paul said it was best not to marry so you can serve with your whole heart. Yet, we know that Paul was married before because of his position within the Sanhedrin, so it would appear he committed himself to the life of the Nazarite after his conversion and marriage.

If this is his position, I am sure he did not imply that everyone should not marry forever, but when you become a widower, it may be a good time to dedicate your life to Yah. Or, maybe he meant to give your best years to Yah like too many of us do with sin. Samuel was given to God at birth, but how many have that story? So few, many question if Jesus (Yashua) was capable of living such a life.

In *Numbers*, it does say you can refrain from being a Nazarite if you go through the actions to remove the calling. This would include cutting your hair and burning it as a wave offering before the Almighty. Samson broke the law of God by cutting his hair, sleeping with unapproved women, and touching dead things. It ought not have been a great shock that Delilah would ultimately betray him.

Samson wanted to be in love like many of us. He wanted what he wanted and never once considered what Yah wanted for him. When he saw the first Philistine woman he decided to marry, he said she was right in his eyes. He did not seek the Lord or appear to give much thought to anyone's opinions.

Judges 14:6-9 ESV

6 Then the Spirit of the Lord rushed upon him, and although he had nothing in his hand, he tore the lion in pieces as one tears a young goat. But he did not tell his father or his mother what he had done.

7 Then he went down and talked with the woman, and she was right in Samson's eyes.

8 After some days he returned to take her. And he turned aside to see the carcass of the lion, and behold, there was a swarm of bees in the body of the lion, and honey.

9 He scraped it out into his hands and went on, eating as he went. And he came to his father and mother and gave some to them, and they ate. But he did not tell them that he had scraped the honey from the carcass of the lion.

It was also right in his own eyes that he ate and shared honey from the carcass of a lion. He knew his parents would have shunned his actions, and so he didn't tell them how he got it. He made the biggest mistake to believe what man could not stop him from doing; Yah wouldn't either. We know that Yah can use vessels of all sorts to accomplish His task. There are no perfect people, and we all fall short of the glory of God. Amazingly, He can use any of us for His great work, is it not?

The Father knew Samson would be a rebellious child because His people were also rebellious. Samson was a product of his environment, and the same was true for King Saul. In government, we are to elect people who best identify with us, our values, and what we believe. In that case, the leaders who rule over the people are to be a reflection of the people's hearts. They were under the Philistine rule because they kept doing what was evil in the sight of Yah, but God also wanted to judge the Philistines (*Judges 13:1*).

Sometimes, it takes crazy to fight crazy. It takes boldness to overcome the proud. It takes confidence to overcome arrogance. Samson was not a perfect man; he was flawed, but the Father sought to use him anyway. Eating honey from the carcass of the dead lion was not right. Choosing a wife, especially one not from his own tribe, was a no, no. In addition, Samson would have appeared to have quite the temper or seed of entitlement.

He didn't ask his parents if he could marry this woman or inquire about their thoughts. He told them what he wanted and expected them to do it without protest. He was used to getting his way and being a single child who was full of expectations, I am sure, made him more entitled.

He took what he wanted and avenged any wrongdoing committed unto him. He was not a ruler who was as much concerned about the people but more so about his own passions, desires, and wants. He offered a riddle to the Philistines, saying that if they solved it, he would give them a prize of 30 men. Only, he chose to go and kill 30 people to give them their prize! What kind of love would make you take life to win your love?

He then sent foxes into their vineyards to tear up their fields because he was upset about being betrayed by the woman he picked! She was trying to spare her own life. She couldn't be loyal to him if that meant she would lose her life and her father's. This love was proven to be very dangerous. After the foxes were released into the field with fire torches that burned up everything, the Philistines responded by burning his wife and her father.

Samson, you would think, would have been satisfied, but his appetite and that of the Philistines grew all the more. His wife was taken from him and given to his best man by her father. Was it love that made him fill with anger or did he feel his manhood was being challenged? They took his woman and uncovered her with another man! This attitude Yah sought to use to demonstrate how He felt against the Philistines. How dare they take from Me what belongs to Me. I will avenge My people.

So in comes Samson, and he kills 1,000 of their

people with the jawbone of a donkey. Keep in mind he had to touch yet another dead animal. Not every servant of the Most High God looks as clean as we want them to be. Who can you use in the prison house but other prisoners to save the lost?

Who could He use in a nation when the ruling power and His people are both on His bad list? No other than a person one would call bad. These are the mysteries that make seeing and understanding Yah a challenge. How could He use a drunk to save the world? We cannot call unclean what the Lord has called clean (*Acts 10:15*).

For 20 years, Samson ruled in the land uncontested, and if contested, he quickly stomped out the threat. Samson ruled, and his people were grateful to Yah that he was there. No, he didn't get it all right, but he got playing his position right for those 20 years. We are so quick to divorce someone because they make mistakes. Aren't we all glad Yah is not like that?

He knew Samson's temper was off, his attitude was not always the best, and he broke laws that made him need to repent. The calling on Samson's life did not change because of his mistakes, but his time frame was cut short because old problems would raise their head in his life again. When Samson was set apart and living the code of the Nazarites, he had peace and safety in the Presence of God.

All was well until the day Samson slept with a Philistine prostitute and exposed his weakness. He had a love for Philistine women. Was it because he liked the thrill of having something he shouldn't? Was it because he liked to spit in the face of his enemy? Or did he just have a thing for Philistine women? One thing is for sure: his love for Philisitine women was the biggest mistake that cost him everything.

Samson was plotted on many of times, but it wasn't until he met and loved Delilah that he was vulnerable enough to be touched by the Philistines. You would think he would have caught on to their scheme. This wasn't his first rodeo, after all with Philistine women. When he told his first wife the riddle, he saw how this woman quickly betrayed him. Why would he risk it all again?

Did he put his faith in his abilities and God's vow to protect him? Why would he lay his head in the lap of the woman he told his weakness, knowing she tested him three times already (*Judges 16:19*)? She drove Samson so crazy about telling her the true source of his strength he was exhausted and bugged to death.

<u>Judges 16:15-16 ESV</u>

15 And she said to him, "How can you say, 'I love you,' when your heart is not with me? You have mocked me these three times, and you have not told me where your great strength lies."

16 And when she pressed him hard with her words day after day and urged him, his soul was vexed to death.

Has anyone put that much pressure on you to change to be with them? They put so much pressure on you to do this, say that, stop talking to this person, and change your schedule or things that are precious to you for them. These changes were often not to make you better but to isolate or weaken you. Why do we choose the people who mean us no good?

She kept nagging until he couldn't take it no more. Imagine if we would allow good things to chase us down and pursue us like we permit the things that harm us. The king gave the mother what she wanted because she came back every day to ask the king. He was so tired of seeing her so he gave her whatever she wanted to keep her from coming back.

Luke 18:1-6 ESV

1 And he told them a parable to the effect that they ought always to pray and not lose heart.

2 He said, "In a certain city there was a judge who neither feared God nor respected man.

3 And there was a widow in that city who kept coming to him and saying, 'Give me justice against my adversary.'

4 For a while he refused, but afterward he said to himself, 'Though I neither fear God nor respect man,

5 yet because this widow keeps bothering me, I will give her justice, so that she will not beat me down by her continual coming.'"

6 And the Lord said, "Hear what the unrighteous judge says.

An unrighteous man granted a petition because he grew tired of hearing the woman. Samson did not have a righteous woman bothering him day in and day out, but a wicked one. She pushed him to do something to his own harm. Have you ever been in a relationship that pushed you to harm yourself?

She didn't sell him out just so she could profit from the money. She knew helping the men who paid her would also equal his death. Did he truly not mean anything to her but a check? How shallow, wicked, and sad for Samson.

He gave his life to a woman who didn't fight for him at all. She knew at least not to be the one who cut his hair. Makes you wonder what she was doing as she watched. Did she keep him comfortable by singing a lullaby to lull him to sleep while she watched the man shave his hair? I also think: How could you not feel your hair being shaved off, though?

How evil of her to watch him at peace in her lap or resting on her knees as she predicted his demise. She not only watched with malicious intent, but she also began to torment him right after his head was shaven.

Judges 16:19-20 ESV

19 Then she lulled him to sleep on her knees, and called for a man, and had him shave off the seven locks of his head. Then [c]she began to torment him, and his strength left him.

20 And she said, "The Philistines are upon you, Samson!" So he awoke from his sleep and said, "I will go out as before, at other times, and shake myself free!" But he did not know that the Lord had departed from him.

Have you noticed when you concede to the will of those who mean you no good, they begin to torment you? They call you stupid, weak, dumb, and pathetic? They say you are good for nothing and not a real man. They say you are a dumb woman they can never marry. They say you are so gullible you would never leave me even if I was the devil himself!

These people get excited to see you crumble before them. They don't mind you hurting. They don't care that their treatment of you causes you pain. They also don't care how their treatment offends you. Samson grew weak after she tormented him.

Have you had a broken spirit before? Has the Presence of Yah left you because you allowed someone else to have a greater importance in your life than God? Have you listened to the theys and ignored the Almighty? Be encouraged!

The conceded heart of these people and the judgment that surely will come to pass if they don't repent is exemplified by Samson and Delilah. Samson, I know, felt betrayed when he was quickly awoken by the voice that frequently did so to warn him the Philistines were coming. He woke up and didn't know the Presence of Yah had already departed from his life. He didn't realize loving this woman slowly killed him, like how King Solomon slowly left God because of women.

This woman humbled him and uncovered the source of his strength. She got into his inner thoughts, feelings, and emotions only to manipulate him. He did not protect his heart and life as he should have. Some of us have shared intimate details with people who told those secrets for fame, new friendships, money, or street credit. How much does your heart sink at that moment you feel the betrayal? Unlike in other times, his strength was not within him to fight or resist the Philistines.

The first thing they did was "put out his eyes." They thought if he couldn't see, he couldn't know the direction in which he was going. They thought a blind mand could put them at no harm or risk. They thought a brokenhearted you would be more controllable than an empowered you. But what they don't know is your hair grows back!

Samson's hair started growing back soon after it was cut. When you are robbed, it is important for you not to lose all hope! When you do something you know you shouldn't have, don't run away from Yah. Don't continue down the downward spiral, but turn away from the broken path. Don't return evil for evil (1 Peter 3:9). Instead, do good works that would be like pouring coals on top of the heads of your enemies (*Proverbs 25:21-22*). Get in right step with

Yah so He can use you again, even as soon as immediately after.

Samson had to come to grips with the error of his ways to pray the right prayer at the right time. He realized he had short-stepped God's plan for his life, and he was quick to repent from it. He asked the Father to forgive him and empower him one more time to give him glory and avenge his betrayal.

The Philistines didn't want to kill him. They wanted to make a mockery of him and use him as an example for any Hebrew who thought to rise up against the Philistines. They wanted to establish their dominance by making Samson their pet to be repeatedly mocked and ridiculed. Samson understood his assignment. He was to be a presence on earth that pointed man back to Yah, especially His children. He was to bring hope and judgment against a people the Father wanted to take vengeance.

Samson was to be the might of Yah's power to be wielded on earth. So he submitted his body if it could be used by Yah and please Him one more time. He was okay with his mistake costing him his life, but he didn't want it to take his purpose. He wanted to give hope to his people. He wanted to do more for them in his death than he did in his life. He wanted to repay them for taking his eyes. The Philistine woman took his eyes off the kingdom, Yah's people, and the purpose of his life.

Judges 16:25-30 ESV

25 So it happened, when their hearts were merry, that they said, "Call for Samson, that he may perform for us." So they called for Samson from the prison, and he performed for them. And they stationed him between the pillars.

26 Then Samson said to the lad who held him by the hand, "Let me feel the pillars which support the temple, so that I can lean on them."

27 Now the temple was full of men and women. All the lords of the Philistines were there—about three thousand men and women on the roof watching while Samson performed.

28 Then Samson called to the Lord, saying, "O Lord God, remember me, I pray! Strengthen me, I pray, just this once, O God, that I may with one blow take vengeance on the Philistines for my two eyes!"

29 And Samson took hold of the two middle pillars which supported the temple, and he braced himself against them, one on his right and the other on his left.

30 Then Samson said, "Let me die with the Philistines!" And he pushed with all his might, and the temple fell on the lords and all the people who were in it. So, the dead that he killed at his death were more than he had killed in his life.

His last request was granted, and he sought justice against those who made fun of not only him but the God he served. They thought that because he was performing before them at their celebration, he was there as a gift from their god. They did not see he was sent there to be a sacrifice unto his own God. Sometimes, we are sent to places to be a light to point to the God we serve. We may have walked into dark places we don't belong, but don't let that stop you from shining Yah's light.

C8
HOSEA'S BOND AND YAH'S MIRRORED MARRIAGE TO A WHORE

Hosea is also a man who knows what it feels like to be asked to do something unorthodox to please the Lord. He was asked to marry Gomer, a woman who would whore herself out, and he would have to take her back! This marriage was to exemplify what Yah felt in connection to His people, but I am sure Hosea asked the question why me?

Why do I have to pick a woman that I know isn't faithful to me? Why must I redeem her, buy her back, when she is the one making mistakes on purpose? He not only bought her back but also had to forgive her and still see her as his wife. He had to choose to take care of other men's children and raise them with his own. (Many scholars have debated on if two children from this marriage were not Hosea's children.) He had to be a single father while his wife left him for the highest bidder.

This was an indecent proposal for sure, but why would a wife make the biggest mistake she could ever make and sin against her own body? Why would she choose to be a man's one-night stand when she has a loving husband committed to her? Why do we choose toxic relationships over the ones that would bless our souls?

Why do we say things like he/she is boring and I can't be with them? Why do we look at trivial things like money to determine who deserves our love, sex, and affection? Why do we say crude comments like his bank account don't make me desire him?

Why do we check someone's social media to see how many likes, friends, and accolades she has to determine how desirable they are? Why do women have to wear everything that is fake to be a real woman? Fake hair, fake nails, fake labels, and walk in fake power to prove she is worthy of your attention. We say we want a real or a down chick, but do many want one that will actually make them better?

Do we today want relationships that will challenge us or pacify our weaknesses and blind spots? Do we want friends that will justify our life choices and explain how our mate doesn't deserve our ratched selves? Have we become so low that the days of Hosea are upon us? We have too many women leaving their families, husbands, and children to chase after men and fame. We have too many willing to be the harlot instead of the wife.

We have too many husbands who don't love their wives enough to support them through anything. So many. If she messes up by talking to him funny, he is out the door, let alone her sleeping with another man. We have become a temperamental generation incapable of real relationships because we want life to come easy. We want following Yah to be easy. We want love, sex, affection, loyalty, and care to be given with no effort.

We would love it if money could be the answer to everything physical and non because we could understand why those with everything should be the happiest. But we see Gomer get what she wants, and it slips through her fingers like running water. We see her constantly being put in a hard place. We see her in a dark place, and her husband comes to her rescue.

Have you met women who ended up in crack-houses, were sex trafficked, or were forced to live a life below what she was called to? Some of them left home willingly in search of a man with wealth who would treat them like a glorified prostitute. No love is there, though. They use them up, drug them up, and leave them for dead in their addictions.

These men don't clean up the messes they leave in her life. They don't care about the children she bears because all of them say it is not theirs. They point fingers and laugh at her, tormenting her to where her spirit is broken like Samson.

She doesn't know how the presence of God has left her life, but she is too weak to fight off the thoughts, the actions, and the addictions that bring her a false sense of security. She performs tricks and allows herself to be the center of attention but receives no affection. She lays her life down on the altar of fallen gods as those who claim to be her friends mock, abuse, and misuse her.

She sees, but she doesn't perceive. She closes her eyes to the pain she feels, and instead of getting angry and seeking vengeance for them taking her vision, hope, and future, she buries herself alive. She can't see her future, and she has no energy to fight, but Hosea comes in and saves her from herself. God sent Gomer an angel to redeem her. To remind her that she is loved and that there is one faithful to her.

Do you think she feels guilty returning home to a good husband with all the wrongs that she had done? Do you think she believes she deserves this relationship? I am sure she saw the stains of her past, the greed of her addiction to artificial things, and also her lust to get them again if her heart was not changed. Her eyes are missing, and she needs a guide. Only the blind keep linking up with the blind, and they both fall into the ditch of the devil's schemes and plans (*Matthew 15:14*).

Gomer had an unquenchable desire for things, a wicked love like Samson, for what doesn't love her back.

Hosea 7:1-7 The Message

1-2

"Every time I gave Israel a fresh start,

wiped the slate clean and got them going again,

Ephraim soon filled the slate with new sins,

the treachery of Samaria written out in bold print.

Two-faced and double-tongued,

  they steal you blind, pick you clean.

It never crosses their mind

  that I keep account of their every crime.

They're mud-spattered head to toe with the residue of sin.

  I see who they are and what they've done.

3-7

"They entertain the king with their evil circus,

  delight the princes with their acrobatic lies.

They're a bunch of overheated adulterers,

  like an oven that holds its heat

From the kneading of the dough

  to the rising of the bread.

On the royal holiday the princes get drunk

  on wine and the frenzy of the mocking

  mob.

They're like wood stoves,

  red-hot with lust.

Through the night their passion is banked;

  in the morning it blazes up, flames hungrily

  licking.

Murderous and volcanic,

>they incinerate their rulers.

Their kings fall one by one,

>and no one pays any attention to me.

Too many are not paying attention to Yah. We are busy getting all we can get from each other but lack an understanding. Gomer would not accept the fresh start that God gave her. Her lust and passion were for the wicked things God despised.

She was like a pig that, after being cleaned, goes back into the mud. She was like the dog that returned to its vomit, mistaking it as good when it already was rejected from her body (*Proverbs 26:11*). What would make someone go back to what has already proven to be against them? What makes men and women so foolish to repeat what has already been rejected?

<u>Hosea 2:2-5 NLT</u>

2 "But now bring charges against Israel—your

>mther—for she is no longer my wife,

>and I am no longer her husband.

Tell her to remove the prostitute's makeup

>from

her face and the clothing that exposes her

>breasts.

3 Otherwise, I will strip her as naked

    as she was on the day she was born.

I will leave her to die of thirst,

    as in a dry and barren wilderness.

4 And I will not love her children,

    for they were conceived in prostitution.

5 Their mother is a shameless prostitute

    and became pregnant in a shameful way.

She said, 'I'll run after other lovers

    and sell myself to them for food and water,

for clothing of wool and linen,

    and for olive oil and drinks.'

Do we not wear the clothes and makeup that more aligns with the world than the healing love of Christ? Do we run after the ways of the fallen instead of worshiping the Almighty King? Do we bow our ideas, hopes, and dreams to look more like the kingdom of hell than heaven? Why do we assume because God used people from every walk of life, He wants us to come and live a fallen life after being raised better?

Children who have known God since birth should look different from those who have never known Him. He has expectations for His children because He wants to use us. How can He use us to be a witness when we are constantly being retrained on the basics? How can you advance the Kingdom when every generation repeats the sins of their parents habitually? It was not only Samuel, Elisha, Elijah, Paul, Stephen, and those now asleep mentioned in the Bible that could please God; we, too, must look at how we can correct ourselves quickly and not wait on the burning bush each time.

If a husband asks his wife to cover up and not wear revealing clothes, these strange women will burst into rage and accuse him of suppression. They call him everything but a child of God and say he is a dictator, oppressor, and slave master. They claim they won't be his slave, but they are a slave to lust, sin, and everything wicked the Father hates. I tell you, this should not be so. How quickly we forget those who love us because we don't want to humble ourselves and take direction.

This is not the fault of the people–only for why they don't know how to be holy anymore. For why people are offended to be ruled by God. It is the fault of the leadership for why women no longer know how to be wives, and young men don't know how to be husbands. When laws were enacted to cause division and reroute a people to live a life contrary to heaven, too many said nothing or ignored it as if it would correct itself.

When checks were written for households without fathers because tithes were still coming, not much judgment was put there. Marriage became optional, covenant became optional, and men left the church! Families broke down, people felt abandoned, and the result was people put their lives and souls in the hands of other men. We have rejected our husband and rightful king to chase after the ways of idolaters. Pastors have more say in too many marriages than the husband.

<u>Hosea 4:4-11 NLT</u>

4 "Don't point your finger at someone else

    and try to pass the blame!

My complaint, you priests,

    is with you.[a]

5 So you will stumble in broad daylight,

    and your false prophets will fall with you in the night.

    And I will destroy Israel, your mother.

6 My people are being destroyed

    because they don't know me.

Since you priests refuse to know me,

    I refuse to recognize you as my priests.

Since you have forgotten the laws of your God,

    I will forget to bless your children.

7 The more priests there are,

    the more they sin against me.

They have exchanged the glory of God

   for the shame of idols.[b]

8 "When the people bring their sin offerings,

   the priests get fed.

So the priests are glad when the people sin!

9 'And what the priests do, the people also do.'

   So now I will punish both priests and people

   for their wicked deeds.

10 They will eat and still be hungry.

   They will play the prostitute and gain nothing

      from it,

   for they have deserted the Lord

11   to worship other gods.

We wonder why tithes don't come into some churches or why the percentage is so low compared to membership numbers. How can people be in church and be unusable for decades on end? Faulty leadership has scared away many believers. Many sheep have run off because their shepherd was wicked or because the righteous were taken, and it takes Yah to redeem them (*Ezekiel 34*). It takes an almighty God to have the heart and mind to seek out his children spread all over, living and believing everything and anything.

We look at relationships today and still don't know where to place the blame. We see men fighting women and women fighting men. We see the confusion in the land, and we don't think for a second that this has something to do with us taking our eyes off the standard. We forget that there is a natural order that has been in place since before time began.

We are quick to throw out the old in exchange for something new. Only we don't know what has intrinsic and lasting value anymore. New technology today is quickly replaced in months because our society is groomed to want the next thing, no matter the simple adjustments. We don't care if much has changed, but life shouldn't slow down. If life slows down, we may think too much or get into more mischief, some believe. But when you run fast or drive a car at a high speed across a short distance, the distance that you pass is blurry.

Your vision is compromised because your eyes don't get the chance to assess anything. Your eyes matter, and where you spend your time, heart, attention, or give your affection matters. Who you choose to marry matters. We need to plead with one another to put away the customs we have accepted to promote whoring after other trains of thought. We have despised the simple things, simple instructions Yah has given us for the complex rules put on us by kings.

We are okay with carrying burdens never meant to be carried by us and lost dominion in every facet of our lives. We have shrunk into the scene, into the communities from which we were sold, to where we no longer are a people set apart for Yah's work. But the nations are waiting for us to take our place in the world. The church must take up its space so that the world may have hope!

Hosea 6:1-3 NLT

1

"Come, let us return to the Lord;

 for he has torn us, that he may heal us;

  he has struck us down, and he will bind us up.

2

After two days he will revive us;

 on the third day he will raise us up,

that we may live before him.

3

Let us know; let us press on to know the Lord;

 his going out is sure as the dawn;

he will come to us as the showers,

 as the spring rains that water the earth."

Has it not come to your mind that the reason we don't know which comes first, the chicken or the egg, is because the Father has permitted our confusion? We don't understand how we drifted so far away from what we used to be in the 1950s to today. Many charts point to a darker future if we keep this path of so-called progression. The Black community had more marriages, wealth, and a sense of community then than they do now. The Negro leagues did more for black communities with their little than any pro athlete since then.

We can't name too many celebrities who have gone to their hoods to do more than prove they made it out. How many have started programs, created grants, built schools, paid for teachers, or brought community back to the community? We should stop this love-and-leave mentality.

It is sad that, too often, people are more concerned about what they can get out of Hollywood for themselves and not what they can bring to bless their own people. We think the work itself is enough, but our communities become bigger ghettos. Poverty grows where some of the best talents have come from. How so?

I wonder how it is possible the people of Congo live in such dire straits when the resources the world needs to create technology are harvested from its lands. How is there a peacekeeping mission updated every 20 years, and no peace ever ensues? How are the peacekeepers paid millions or billions of dollars, and no results are required?

How is it possible the French can mandate prior colonized African nations to bank with them and then charge them interest to borrow their own money? How is Haiti struggling when a precious metal native to the land because of a meteor strike is harvested from there? How is anybody poor in the nation when millions and billions of dollars are made worldwide off their poverty?

South Africa also has jewels native only to their lands, and their dollar is worth pennies compared to the West, but how? How is the currency of many nations with raw materials valued at such a lopsided number as the West when everything comes from the East and is brought West and then sold back to the East at a premium? Is this not evil?

Many designers stole graphics and images from these people and sold them back at a premium. They tell these people their brands are better, that only their brands are their culture wrapped in fabric! How are there no laws protecting their precious materials and intellectual property? How are their secrets found out and put in movies for the world to watch, and the theys don't compensate or acknowledge the people for their contribution? How is that justice, fair, and balanced?

The world uses humanity's ignorance against itself. When you have a lover that doesn't love you back, it hurts. When you love a conditioned belief more than the truth, it hurts. When we went awhoring after other nations' ways, governments, practices, or ways to earn money, we lost our way.

Moses's people went chasing after money to be made in the temples and forsake their position in God. Their empty post cost the nation and, ultimately, cost them their freedom. Gomer wasn't present in her marriage because she was too busy comparing her husband to other men she thought were better.

Many women and men can't be happy because they don't know how to appreciate what they already have. People want a new king because they don't know the king they already have! The Hebrews have the King of King and God of all Creation as their king, and they still compare His precepts, rules, and ways to those of mere men. It is a sad day when His people side with men over Him.

These people, same as us, forget too often that He is a Jealous God (*Exodus 20:5*). He brought the Gentiles to worship and honor Him to make His people jealous (*Romans 11:4*). Yashua called a Gentile a dog in *Matt 15:21-28*, but she was not offended but humbled herself and said, even the dogs eat the crumbs off the Master's table!

How many of us would not bow our heads to anything God says because we are a stiff-neck people? We are worse than Pharoah. We don't see that our path is leading us to destruction, and we don't mind that our dreams are devoid of fulfillment. We know that chasing certain careers can put us in the hands of the devil and many don't have a plan of escape.

They don't plan to follow Yah's way to expand the kingdom; they simply jump aboard the train and head for hell. We don't have to be consumed to have a seat at the table. But if that is the case, we have to be willing to step away from the table and do a new thing.

If we want to know what will restore our marriages, our people, the nations, and the world, it is the steadfast love and not sacrifice that pleases Yah.

Hosea 6:6-7 NLT

6 For I desire steadfast love[a] and not sacrifice,

the knowledge of God rather than burnt offerings.

7 But like Adam they transgressed the covenant;

there they dealt faithlessly with me.

It does not please God that we turn our back on His knowledge to gain wealth that we think to give as an offering to bless Him. It makes no effect to Him that you make money doing things He finds deplorable. He doesn't want your things. He desires your obedience more than your sacrifice.

He doesn't want you to go out here in search of a perfect man or woman. He wants you to be obedient to a covenant you make with someone who is a part of your purpose. Imperfect people are in marriages that must learn to work together to become one flesh.

We don't get there by abandoning each other or running away when we are hurt by each other. We don't get brownie points by pointing to our spouse's weaknesses and exposing his/her bed to others for high-fives. We don't give Yah glory by functioning like the world and engaging in the things the world says are cool.

We bring shame to the legacy He built through King David when we don't have a heart set on living for Him. When we act as if there is nothing we can or should work on, when we are rude, nasty, unfaithful, inconsistent, or inappropriate, we lose our way. Inch by inch, we sold our solid foundation. It's time to put our two feet on solid ground and allow the Father to redeem us.

We need Him to bring us back from the strip clubs, being whoremongers, absent parents, lustful, money hungry, working to death, being a narcissist, lying, stealing, killing, and speaking hateful words to each other. We need Yah to reroute our minds, hearts, and will to conform to what He always had in mind for us. Yes, we make mistakes, but He desires a steadfast love that doesn't shift like the weather.

He wants a people where He can be their God, King, and Husband. He is a keeper of those who rest in His hands, and for those who do, no one can pluck you out. There is protection and provision, even the ability to do what you feel you can't. It would surely take Yah for Hosea to redeem a wife like Gomer. It takes a God like this to redeem a people like us! Redeem a world like ours! To give a Son to exemplify truth and hope for us!

So, yes, God can redeem the value of a prostitute. To redeem the value of a lost generation, restore broken relationships, and heal relationships including our connection to Him. He wants us to come to Him with everything and be faithful to our assignment. He wants us to stop starting and stopping but to keep running in the faith. If you need grace, it is here, but don't live in iniquity and claim that it is your best.

He wants us to be men and women after His own heart, like King David. He wants us to acknowledge our shortcomings and bring them to Him. He doesn't expect us to come clean but dirty, broken, and in need of a Savior. He is our deliverer, our peace, rest, hope, and future. As He works on us, He is expecting and demanding change. You cannot encounter God and not be changed.

Anyone who says they know Yah and are comfortable living in sin, they deceive themselves and are a thief and a liar. These people will try to enter his banquet without changing their clothes and will be tossed out, where teeth will be gnashed (*Matthew 22*). These people reject the Gospel or treat it like the sons of Eli who were judged.

Don't make this mistake!

FOLLOW

C9

A PEOPLE AFTER
YAH'S OWN
HEART

Someone that keeps coming up like a jack in the box is King David. He's the man with fabulous stories about his relationship and unshakable faith in Yah. For just as many powerful testimonies he has, King David seems to also have dark moments. I am sure if we look over our lives, we can see moments of darkness. Things we have done or thought to do that would put us in any social doghouse and rightfully out of heaven!

Yet this fallible man had a place in Yah's heart that didn't shift when he failed. When he messed up time and time again, there was something about David that made the Father have mercy. Although we cannot be sure as to why Yah has mercy where He chooses, I love that He does!

How much more do we need to learn to be honest about our shortcomings like David? David knew when he messed up and was so quick to bring his error before God for forgiveness and judgment if need be. He never hid from Yah, even when he may have wanted to after taking a man's wife and seeing the birth of his first son. He knew the baby was going to die, but oh! on that day, he wished he could have hidden his sin. But he didn't run away from God; he ran to Him.

He mourned the life of his son and spent that time with Yah and allowed Him to restore his heart. God was always sending King David's help. He sent Jonathan when he started his rise as king. When he thought of backing down from pursuing his future, Jonathan encouraged him to keep going a second time.

How many of us want to turn around when we hit opposition? We think maybe this isn't for me, maybe I misheard, or I should retreat and come back later. I know I used to feel like the battles I faced were a sign that I should retreat. I kept retreating, backing off, and starting over. Have you found whatever the Father put in you to do, you come back to after some time?

Sometimes, it is in our thoughts that we remember, and other times, we repeat the action as before, picking up where we left off or starting over. Only if we quit again will we find that we have not reached the promised land because we got intimidated like the Hebrews when the scouts gave their report. If we focus on our shortcomings, how short we are, how ill-prepared we are, etc., we forget that we have the Almighty Yah on the inside of us.

We all need an angel to be sent our way to give us a word when we feel discouraged.

Samson's mother asked the angel to come back and tell her husband so she could have a witness for what she heard. It's okay if you need to hear your purpose not once but twice. It's okay if you started, had to stop, or chose to stop, and now you have to do it again.

Remember when the disciples were fishing all night and caught nothing? Yashsua told them to cast the net again on the other side of the boat, and so much flew at them that they needed help carrying the load (*Matthew 4:8-22*)!

Sometimes, we have to go at something again and not give up, like how Hosea couldn't give up on Gomer. Even more important is how Yah doesn't give up on us. We learn patience, forgiveness, and what it means to serve in this kingdom when we can hear a yes and a no; likewise, when we can hear a compliment or a rebuke.

Don't allow yourself to get so high in your head to where no one can tell you anything. Don't be like Samson, and put your power in your abilities because when your power fades, you will find yourself hoping you can call out to God, and He will hear you. Don't take His presence for granted like King Saul. Don't think that because you have this authority to rule, you can be disobedient with no consequences.

If you mess up, own your mistakes and take accountability like King David. When we own our faults and sincerely repent from our ways to adopt Yah's, we can get into right standing with Him. When we are like Pharoah and allow God to show us something, we can receive a prize that we never deserve. When we humble ourselves like Gomer and go home, we can find rest just as the prodigal. I am sure she got dirty looks from people who knew her faults, but to the one her faults mattered the most, he chose to leave them in the past and forgive.

I want you to know no matter what mistakes you have made; if you are here with breath in your lungs, you can choose to make the best decision that can give you everything! The Bible says, "**Seek first the kingdom of God and his righteousness, and all these things will be added unto you** (*Matthew 6:33*)."

We have to learn to value the things of Yah more than we care for the things created by man. We have to value what God considers decent and modest. We have to see how we are to love our husband or wife according to what He says. Should your husband be able to talk to you about exposing your breasts to the world? The world may tell you, "No, because it is your body." Yah says, "**Yes, because your body is no longer your own when married** (*1 Corinthians 7:4*)."

Some may say that I am single, so I can do what I want until I get married. The Bible says,

1 Timothy 2:9-10 ESV

9 likewise also that women should adorn themselves in respectable apparel, with modesty and self-control, not with braided hair and gold or pearls or costly attire,

10 but with what is proper for women who profess godliness—with good works.

Nope, this applies to you too. If you are a godly woman you should not only look like it, but your actions should confirm it. Why is it important how you live your life, what you look like, or how you treat others?

The world is watching you. Children are watching you. We are to set the standard for what it is like to follow a God like this. We are to exemplify what Yah can do with broken, discarded, and undesirable vessels. We are to prove people wrong every day who say Yah can't by demonstrating HE has!

God is not dead, but He is alive, living on the inside of His children and using them no matter their condition to advance His Kingdom on earth. He wants to make us ambassadors, brand ambassadors, that demonstrate the goodness of His kingdom to all mankind. King David proved God's goodness to make a perfect being come from the legacy of a man with flaws.

He clothed His Word in Flesh and honored His promise to make David a king forever! What promises has Yah given you? What promises has He given to your family? What will you allow Him to do with your life and family? He can do more than bless you with a healthy relationship, money, a house, and cars. He has so much more for those who love Him and are called according to His purpose (*Romans 8:28*).

Is it okay if He calls your name to stand up for Him right where you are? He can use you like you are now and still finish a work He starts in you (*Philippians 1:6*). He can use you throughout your journey. You don't have to become perfect to then be used. You can come broken, confused, rejected, hurt, vengeful, hateful, made, and ungrateful. The Father knows how to turn hearts toward Him. He knows how to win souls. He just wants you to be faithful to serve.

I pray that all men and women who Yah approaches to work for His kingdom accept the invitation and allow Him to step into every area of their lives. We are victorious when we are tested and do as Yah has instructed us. We are helping when we are for Him and don't stand against Him (*Mark 9:38-41*). You don't have to know everything or be everywhere, but you want to be faithful and renew your mind, will, and emotions to that of Yah.

I would like to leave you with a prayer. Like everyone in this book, we have all made big mistakes, and for some of us, it cost us everything! Then, for others, it was an opportunity for us to know we needed to get right with Yah the Almighty and True God. If this is a time that you know you should get right with Yah, I want to pray with and for you.

"Father, may You touch the life, heart, and mind of every reader touched by this book. May You open their eyes and heart to see who they are and what they need to do to start a relationship with You. May You teach them that they are valuable to You no matter their current condition. Show them that they can be used to advance the kingdom on earth, starting with their own life. May you give them the strength to see the plans You have for them. May the enemy no more steal their hope, joy, and future.

May you restore the time they lost chasing after things, people, or ideals that were not profitable. May they see You in everything they do. May they no longer have a stony heart or prickled mind that no one can reach. May You give them a heart of flesh to care about the things and people You care about. May they no longer be caught up in their own feelings but considerate of Your thoughts, ways, and purpose.

We thank You, Father, for Your Word, Your Son, the messiah, Yahshua, the Christ who died for our sins. He died so that we may be restored to a connection with You. Father, I pray my sister or brother is willing to confess that Yahshua is the Son of Yah, the Word wrapped in flesh. He is the eternal sacrifice that allows man and the Almighty God to be reconnected.

May they start this journey of discovery, growing closer to you each day. It is in Your son's name, Yahshua, that we say thank You and hallelujah!"

Your Sister, Dr. Lee

ABOUT THE
AUTHOR

K. Lee is a strong believer in prayer and believes the Truth sets anyone free. She is grateful that the Almighty has come into her life and removed her from a path of self-destruction to one that keeps her heart, mind, and desire to help the masses. As a child, she wanted to be light-hearted and not wear her heart on her sleeves or not cry when she saw others cry. This, however, was not the way the Lord made her.

The Lord called Krystal to have a heart that cares for others, sympathizes with the afflicted, and seeks justice or help for the needy. K. Lee is passionate about projects that build up people, remove oppression and pain, and deliver hope. Her childhood ambitions were to express her thoughts and those of the silent in music, dance, theater, and especially in writing.

K. Lee has written over 30 books and has a goal to publish at least 50 or more! Her books are both fiction and non-fiction, spanning seven genres: adult, children, youth fiction, self-help, spiritual growth, novels, business, empowerment, etc., to help people in their most profound times of need.

She is also passionate about coaching programs and web courses she created for WAE (Write Anything Easily) Process, Embrace Your Crown, Turn Key Solution for Small and New Businesses, Transform Go Beyond Change (Personal Development, and The Lesson for

Youth and Teenagers.

In addition to writing books, K. Lee is passionate about video and media production. She started writing music and then transitioned to screenplays and theater. K. Lee is a talented actress who prefers to be behind the scenes.

Dr. Lee is equally passionate about ministry as she is about commerce, entertainment, and writing. She enjoys teaching and speaking on subjects relative to her life experience and anointed ability. She believes God has a calling on her life to be a mouthpiece for Him; she is prepared to follow His voice and travel to where He sends her without the slightest hesitation.

K. Lee hates religion, spreading faith through fear, and believes in the value of men no matter the current condition. No one is beyond the healing hand of Yahweh if they want the help. Help can be offered but must always be accepted, which requires choice. Yahshua is her Lord and Savior, and she looks forward to His coming. The days we live in remind her that The Second Coming is growing near. She believes and is passionate about helping all who have an ear to hear the Good News!

If you would like to learn more about K. Lee (Dr. Lee) or order more of her published books, you can find her online using the information below.

FB, TW, IG Pages: @AuthorKLee
AuthorKLee.com
DrKrystalLee.com
Me@DrKrystalLee.com
me@AuthorKLee.com

AuthorKLee.com
Creator of
WAE Process

     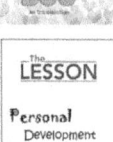

SCAN ME

Call or Text:
770-240-0089 Press Extension 1
Web: KLEpub.com
Email Services@klepub.com

It's time to start and finish   **YOUR Story!**

KLE Publishing specializes in helping people become authors. In as little as 15 to 90 days, we can help you develop your books and e-books and publish to 39,000 outlets! We also offer audiobook services.

Write, Edit, Format, Publish
We can help from
Start to Finish.

Explore and learn more about published authors affiliated with KLE.

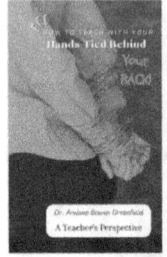

KLEPub.com

www.ingramcontent.com/pod-product-compliance
Lightning Source LLC
Chambersburg PA
CBHW072016110526
44592CB00012B/1330